Sierra Leone Higher Education:
At the Crossroads of Change

Kosonike Koso-Thomas

With the compliments of the author

Koso Thomas

Sierra Leonean Writers Series

Sierra Leone Higher Education:
At the Crossroads of Change

ISBN: 978-9988-8698-5-4

First published in Kindle
by
Nyakon Publishing (www.nyakon.com)
Great Britain in 2012.

This edition by

Sierra Leonean Writers Series (SLWS)
Warima/Freetown/Accra
120 Kissy Road, Freetown, Sierra Leone
Publisher: Osman Sankoh (Mallam O.)
publisher@sl-writers-series.org

This book is dedicated to my wife, Yinka.
During the difficult days of the struggle to achieve change in a setting unprepared for it, it was her encouragement and support that kept me focussed on that primary objective.

Contents

Chapter	Description	Page
	Dedication	i
	Contents	ii
	Acknowledgements	iv
	Foreword	vi
	Preface	vii
1	Level of Traditional Science and Technology in Middle Africa	1
	Early Societies and Techniques	3
	Science and Technology in the Colonial Period	7
2	Background to Sierra Leone's Higher Education	13
3	State of National Science and Technology in Sierra Leone at the dawn of Independence	18
4	Fourah Bay College and its Environs	26
5	The Early Days of as a Disciipline at Fourah Bay College	36
	Initiating Policy Change	36
	Planning Changes to Old Courses	48
6	Implementing the new Diploma in Engineering Courses	60
	Overcoming initial challenges	60
	Annual Academic Standards Review at the University of Durham	65
	Students Admission and Preferential Scholarships for Science and Engineering Applicants	69
	Overcoming Prejudice against Course Offering	70
7	Establishing Full Degree Courses in Engineering	77
	Minor Setbacks; New Opportunities	77

	Further Expansion and Staff Development	85
8	Creating a National Structure for Engineering Education	93
	Rationalizing the Engineering Education System	93
	Compromise Programme responding to failure to implement United Structure	104
9	Founding of the Faculty of Engineering	102
	Upgrading Degree Courses	104
	Preparation for the final stages of Transition	110
10	The Faculty of Engineering Today	112
	Organization Structure of the Faculty	112
	Entry Requirements into the Faculty	112
	Courses offered and Stucture	113
	Post-Graduate Trainng at the Faculty	114
	Prospects and Responsibilities	**115**
11	The Slow March towards Change	117
	Expections of Facilities and Programmes	117
	Vision and Drive towards the Training of Architects	118
	Navigating the undulating road to the training of Mining Engineers	128
	Curriculum Revision and Re-Structuring of Faculty Programme	133
12	Development and Prosperity: The Chalenges for Sierra Leone	135
	References	146
	Notes	149
	Revised Undergraduate Degree Programmes in the Faculty of Engineering and Architecture	149
	Index	155

Acknowledgements

I gratefully acknowledge the support and encouragement of my wife, Olayinka, during my years of service at Fourah Bay College and during the preparation of the manuscript.

This story would not have been possible without the support of some of my colleagues who worked tirelessly with me to achieve the changes that have transformed the lives of many young people. However, the following deserve special mention:

Professor Nicholas J Garber, former Dean of Engineering at Fourah Bay College and presently Henry L. Kinnier Professor Emeritus at the Civil and Environmental Engineering, Department of the University of Virginia, in the United States of America and Dr. Shola Chinsman, former Senior Lecturer in the Department of Civil Engineering at Fourah Bay College and former United Nations Resident Representative to Nigeria. Both Professor Garber and Dr. Chinsman provided valuable comments and advice during the final stages of preparation of this book.

I also acknowledge the contributions of the following people:

Ing. Alex & Mrs (Dr.) Moira Browne, Mr. Ainah Atere-Roberts, Ing. Nikyn Koso-Thomas, Professor Eldred & Mrs Marjorie Jones, and Dr Francis Nicol for reading the manuscript and making necessary corrections to the text. Also, Mr. Alex D. S. Williams for his assistance in searching old documents and photographing many of the sites referred to in the book, and Dr. Wilfred Wright for his valuable work in mounting the photographs and for his suggestions regarding the publishing of the manuscript.

Ing A. Badami Savage, former Dean of the Faculty of Engineering and Architecture, and Arch. Alpha Tejan-Jalloh, Partner in the firm of TEDA Sierra Leone, provided valuable information on new developments in the faculty, which has now been transformed under the leadership of Dean Savage. The section on 'The Faculty

Today' would not have been so detailed, without reference to the notes they made available for use in preparing this section of the book. Their contribution is greatly appreciated.

Foreword

Although Fourah Bay College, since its foundation in 1827, had played a singular role in the education and enlightenment of generations of West Africans, and had contributed to the growth of the civil and religious institutions of the region, it was not until the early 1950s that engineering began to take its place in its intellectual life and influence. Engineering was fortunate in that its introduction into the curriculum of the College, first as the protégé of the Faculty of Pure & Applied Science, coincided with the recruitment of young Sierra Leoneans, to help shape its courses and ensure its relevance to the needs of the country. One such lecturer led the planning of the early non-degree courses and handed over these firm formative plans to the first expatriate head of the department. But it was Kosonike Koso-Thomas, this same young man, now Professor, who was once again in charge when the department attained full faculty status and popularized engineering education among school children as well as opened the facilities of the Faculty to the nation.

His authentic history reveals that this progress was not without difficulties and setbacks which were, however, fortunately overcome. Perhaps the most striking fruit of his vision is the popularity of Engineering among women who are now visible along with their male counterparts, in strategic technical positions.

It was always my pleasure as Principal of the College to go on my own or take visitors to this vigorous faculty engaged in research projects directly related to the future needs of Sierra Leone.

Eldred Durosimi Jones

Preface

Human capacity building is one of the key pillars on which the development and prosperity of a nation rest. Its strength, however, is derived from a complex set of factors relating to education and training of manpower. Early strategies applied by various governments in Sierra Leone, following independence from Britain, underestimated the investments required in education and training, particularly in the engineering fields, to achieve sound economic growth and prosperity. There is a direct relationship between capacity building and institution strengthening, in the sense that weak institutions cannot build strong manpower capacities. Furthermore, institutions starved of funds to undertake their vital roles in manpower training cannot produce the manpower requirements for economic development and prosperity. Thus, engineering manpower as a component of the productive cycle of any nation, must be trained in institutions where the quality of the products is not jeopardised by inadequate funding or internal prejudices. Only through the production of well trained engineering and technical personnel, could a nation expect to benefit from a progression of technical advancement from one generation to another, enriching the social and material lives of all citizens.

In the early 1960s, light industries were beginning to appear in urban centres in the country, joining the mineral extractive industries that had earlier been established in the rural areas. Yet, training institutions in Sierra Leone were unable to supply the calibre of personnel required to fill vacancies at the senior technical levels. Most of these vacancies had to be filled by personnel trained overseas, only a few of whom were Sierra Leoneans. It had been obvious for a long time that the poor planning strategies and lack of commitment from government to provide the resources that were required, prevented existing institutions from taking advantage of those past opportunities. The decision, taken in 1954, to introduce engineering as a discipline at Fourah Bay College, an affiliate of Durham University, began a new chapter in the educational history of the country. It showed that the country was then ready to correct the weaknesses in the institutional arrangements for manpower training in the country. The university took the challenge and prepared itself for the first steps towards the local training of the country's professional engineers.

Kosonike Koso-Thomas

Chapter 1
Level of Traditional Science and Technology in Middle Africa

The issue of the level of science and technology in Africa has been a topic of debate among academics in the region since the dawn of independence from the colonial powers. Many of them believe that the region was being left behind in the race to acquire and master the elements of science and technology that would place it in the mainstream of world development in the modern world. It has become clear that participation in these activities comes not by chance, but from structured education and training in the sciences, and a continued investment in research and the development of fundamental ideas in all branches of the sciences.

In many countries of the region, the major setback to involvement in any form of scientific development has been the failure to establish scientific and technological institutions early enough in their history to permit the gradual transformation of traditional skills, through the application of scientific methods. Many reasons have been given for this failure, not least, is the fact that the region, particularly those territories south of the Sahara, was isolated from the centres of civilization in the north, where the seeds of modern science and technology were sown. Sub-Saharan Africa remained the dark region and for centuries, stayed exploited for labour and materials that fuelled the technological development of countries in the northern hemisphere. Whatever the elements of science and technology taking place in that sub-region before it emerged from isolation and uncontrolled exploitation, it stayed largely unknown to the rest of the world.

As a result, it was imagined that the peoples in that region basked in primitiveness and ignorance in the sunshine and rainstorms of a forsaken continent until European explorers discovered them, and brought them the blessings of civilized living.

1

We now know that Africa is the home of man and that some ancient civilizations flourished there, before the advent of western civilization. Even during the Middle Ages, while Western Europe was suffering general decay under feudalism, great empires were flourishing in Africa. It is quite clear that these empires could not have supported organized social, economic, and political life without the development of well entrenched technological systems within the structure and limitations of the demands of those societies.

It has become a complex issue today, however, to deal with matters relating to Africa as though Africa possessed a monolithic racial structure. It has often been emphasized by older European writers that of the two distinct racial groups that inhabited the continent before the advent of the Europeans, those who lived in the South of the Sahara had little or no heritage. These writers believed, therefore, that the early scientific and technological achievements of the Egyptians, the Moors, and the Berbers in the north could not be claimed by all of Africa. They ignored the evidence of the achievements of the Bantu and other cultures to the south, attributing them to foreign influences. Whatever the issues are today which separate the black 'belt' of Middle Africa from the rest of the world, they no longer ostensibly include racial issues. Happily, also, the preposterous suggestion current in the early fifties that the black man is a comparatively recent inhabitant of Africa, has been rejected several times. Newer and more reputable scholarly works have produced evidence which positively suggest that every region of Africa, including Egypt and the North-Western reaches of the Sahara, once possessed thriving black populations. Therefore, the record of the achievements of North Africa, including those of the Ancient Egyptians, from their great skill in irrigation and farming, to their remarkable architectural talents shown in the building of the pyramids along the Nile, and other magnificent edifices like Pharaohs' tombs; from their discovery of the processes for embalming their dead, to the great invention of the art of writing; from their inventions in science, to those in

2

mathematics and medicine; all these are part of the black man's heritage.

However, the origin and development of science and technology in Middle Africa, the area many writers refer to as that belt south of the Sahara and north of South Africa, is not well known. Even modern African historians have reserved only the most grudging commentary on the systems and methods employed by its inhabitants for eking a livelihood, and creating the basis for their enjoyment of life. Yet, it is this region which produced examples of those arts and culture, so striking and rich in their dimensions that the world has had to recognize and accept them as being unsurpassed in their generation by any other peoples anywhere.

Unfortunately, in the excitement and enthusiasm over these cultural discoveries, many historians overlooked the probability of the existence of correspondingly strong supporting technologies and so failed to investigate them. That failure is partly responsible for the slow growth of science and technology in the region.

Early Societies and Techniques

As early as the Seventh century B.C., advanced civilizations and cultures existed among the people of Axum in Eastern Africa and a little later, rose the Kingdom of Ethiopia. By the Christian era, Zimbabwe had grown and was flourishing in the south, whilst the opulence of Ghana was attracting the attention of Arab scholars. The Mali empire, Ghana's successor, reached its peak of splendour and grandeur in the early fourteenth century, possessing a distinct architectural tradition and university education. Other civilizations followed, like Songhai, the Hausa States, Benin, and Ife in the West, each leaving its mark on the history of the area.

In these empires, several reported physical features testify to the existence of practices, albeit unsophisticated, of techniques which helped to create and maintain the grandeur and style of living of the period. The writings of El Idrisi [1] give a vivid description of the

Royal Palace of the rulers of Ghana, which had halls and walls adorned with sculptures, paintings, and glass windows. These writings also tell of townships in the Empire which had been solidly built of clay bricks and stone and in which successful activities were carried out in the production of wool, cotton and silk.

Excavations have confirmed that many of these earlier empires and states also enjoyed the benefits of fine craftsmanship in iron, gold, copper, and jewels, and produced good quality textiles. These activities had a strong raw material base industry in mining and in agriculture. Power was supplied using animals which were a great advantage in wet forest lands. Nevertheless, severe setbacks were experienced in developing labour-saving methods in agriculture, in view of the denseness of the vegetation and the problems of weather and disease, which adversely affected the rearing of cattle and horses. Many of the inhabitants who had migrated to the forest zones from homelands in the Savannah belt, could not easily operate the plough, so they devised manual methods for cultivation in which the axe, the cutlass and the hoe featured as principle implements. As knowledge was acquired and improved for the extraction and working of metals, these implements gradually became fashioned in metal, principally iron.

It is difficult to assert, without qualification, that all the metallurgical skills for smelting and forging of iron, copper, and bronze, acquired by these people over the centuries evolved from them. It is now known that there were parallel developments elsewhere. Nevertheless, quite impressive works in iron, for example, have been attributed to craftsmen of Meroe in modern Sudan, which has been described by archaeologists as the "Birmingham" of black Africa. Development of techniques of this kind is difficult to trace, but changes in methods to bring about improvement in quality of products, if not to reduce the element of manual labour, must have taken place. For this, outside influence may have been an important factor. In the field of metallurgy, influences are likely from the Moors who dominated the trans-Saharan trade for quite a long time. The Moors had made great strides in metallurgy by discovering

4

methods of utilizing sulphide ores of copper from which copper sulphate was obtained and which in turn was dissolved in water and run over iron to produce pure copper. These black people who were the indigenous inhabitants of North Africa before the Arab Conquests of the 7th and 11th Centuries A.D., transmitted ideas and exchanged commodities between West and North Africa through trading activities.

In the growing of crops, there was a gradual adjustment of patterns and skills to provide food for large concentrations of population. Selective cultivation of food crops was developed, the first evidence of which was found in the Niger Valley. This selectivity established crops which were suited to the environment and whose yields satisfied the requirements of the community. Without chemicals and fertilizers, systematized agricultural processes were evolved for enriching the soil after cultivation. The modern terminologies of "crop rotation" and "shifting cultivation", now applied to some of these processes, had their roots deep in the history of these African lands.

Other techniques were practised to a high degree of perfection and indicated the existence of a strong cumulative knowledge about nature. The early Ethiopians, in their efforts to understand the functioning of the universe, gave the stars of the heavens names used today in Astronomy. Several other peoples in the Middle African belt have interpreted stellar phenomena and used them to direct their activities in agriculture, and to assist in the curing of certain human diseases.

Herbal medicines were widely used and herbalists became quite sophisticated in the application of their skills, of which, it is fair to say that their knowledge and skills progressed. Through this development, they were successful in the treatment of conditions, which remain incurable by western medicine. Some of these herbal and other medical cures are retained, and in use to this day for the treatment of difficult cases in orthopaedic surgery, ophthalmology and gynaecology, and have led the way to the development of certain aspects of modern medicine. Inoculation as a means of immunizing people against contracting diseases, is also an ancient skill now adopted by the modern epidemiologist.

Architectural and building practices in early African societies, indicate that certain basic elements of geometry were employed in creating building structures. The massive round towers of the Zimbabwe ruins and other features of famous ruins elsewhere testify to this fact.

Evidence of productive techniques can also be seen in the traditions of dyeing and textile manufacture, which are well known in West Africa and which have survived to this day. It has been established that the loom was an important equipment of local origin. Its invention and development were stimulated by the need of the people for the types of clothing, which gave protection against the weather and insects. The need to provide some touch of glamour for the women and an aura of dignity and splendour for the rulers, caused further improvements to design and quality.

Dyeing has a long history in this area. Dyes were originally made from leaves of plants and barks of trees. Permanency of colours was attained using salt, and extraction of dyes was by a manual process which does not appear to have changed to this day.

It has been suggested that although the manufacture of clothing took place locally in the pre-colonial period, the importance of the industry could only have been marginal since, in Middle Africa, most the population was either sparsely dressed or not dressed at all. A clarification of the position is given by Fyle and Abraham [2] in their studies of the country-cloth culture of Sierra Leone. They explain it as follows:
'The industry was thriving and was an effective technological and economic enterprise. The standard of manufacture was quite high and never failed to impress travellers. In terms of durability, quality, variety, and brightness of colours, and in terms of the artistry of the patterns woven, the cloths were first-rate. There was also evidence

6

that some improvement in the design of the looms took place over a period, resulting in the increase of cloth strip size from fifteen centimetres to about thirty centimetres. There is no doubt, therefore, that the incentive existed to stimulate technical improvement of the earlier primitive weaving implements. This incentive arose not only from the demand for wearing apparel, but also from the common use of country cloths as blankets, hammocks, and tapestry and, most importantly, as a currency for trade and discharge of debts'.

The foregoing analysis makes the case that Middle Africa did possess technological systems and skills which were indigenous to the area, and which contributed to the greatness of the early empires. It is a sad fact to accept today, that several of these systems and skills vanished with the civilizations they so ably supported. By the time the industrial revolution had taken root in Western Europe, European explorers had identified the most promising lands for colonial exploitation. That sequence of events denied Middle Africa its grip on any ordered development of those early technologies. Sadly also, some of their roots were lost in the devastations that accompanied civil wars. Many more disappeared during the disruption, meanness, and brutality, of the Slave Trade. What remained finally succumbed to the impact of colonial restrictions.

Science and Technology in the Colonial Period

Prior to the colonial period, the interior regions of West and Central African States had developed early trade links with the North African States and, through them, with Europe. These links arose out of the need for exchange of each other's commodities.

Interest in reaching the area from the coast, however, was not keen initially. Some interest was shown by the Phoenicians, who were said to have reached the West African coast from the Suez in early times. About 470 B.C. Carthaginians attempted a visit and it is believed that they set up a Carthaginian trading colony at Kerne.

7

The Greeks also visited the area around 200 B.C, but accounts of European contact with the West African coast indicate that the Portuguese were probably the first most important traders, obtaining African gold and ivory which were commercially attractive to them. They also had religious motives for establishing connections with the area. Eventually, time revealed that they were more interested in trade than in spreading Christianity. Their dealings in cheap slave-labour exposed their profanity and brought shame to the religion, whose banner they carried high unto the continent of Africa. The goods which were exchanged for gold, ivory and slaves were later to be recognized as the chief elements which, like the Slave Trade itself, commenced the progressive stifling of traditional technological activities.

When the colonialists arrived, the pattern of the old coast trade was rudely shattered as colonialism itself implied a total abrogation of African sovereignty. This was not always passively accepted by the Africans, but it ushered in the period of dependence as the colonies became grafted to the periphery of the capitalist system. The colonial pattern was strictly set; rigid rule, curtailment of the powers of traditional rulers, exploitation of local resources and provision of markets for European goods. As new sources of local wealth were discovered and exploited, more new and varied products of European origin and craftsmanship were imposed upon the population in exchange for them. Separation of the ruling colonial class from the indigenous population, provided the opportunity for the creation of a community, whose life style was dominated by products, which the indigenous masses were gradually taught to regard as symbols of a superior and desirable culture. Only those scientific and technological activities were introduced, which were related to the improvement of methods for the economic exploitation of cash crops and minerals and for the maintenance of those technologies which supported the lifestyles of the metropolitan countries, localized in the colonial administrator. Through these activities, however, some marginal stimulus was given to the improvement of local craftsmanship and of local scientific capacity. The Colonial Administrations were unable to identify any local expertise upon which they could rely, and so proceeded to equip locally recruited labour with the minimum knowledge required for their efficient functioning within the colonial system. As a result, craft practice was introduced to selected recruits as an introduction to the presumed inexplicable methods of European technology. These newly acquired skills, together with the tools associated with them, quickly took roots in the society and influenced even the practice of certain traditional technologies.

It was never the intention of the colonial powers to advance their subjects towards a better life. Colonial administrators were forbidden to do anything that would add to the responsibilities and expense of the Colonial Administration. So, in terms of improved technological skills, Middle Africa crawled at a snail's pace under the yoke of colonialism and imperialism from the late nineteenth century to the third quarter of the twentieth century. Within the limitations of the period, however, the local craftsmen, through their own initiative and resourcefulness, applied the skills they had learnt through contact with their new rulers, to make imitations of European devices, implements and products, which they felt were useful for the betterment of their own lives. There was of course, the lack of knowledge of quantitative principles for obtaining exact proportions and strength of components of products made. Nevertheless, these craftsmen produced household goods which included the safety iron and the "Coal Pot", some agricultural implements and even guns.

In this way, the products of western science seeped through communities detached from the abstractions of scientific analysis from which they were derived. A theoretical base was never established for these skills and consequently little or no quantitative expression for applying then was known. Because of this, those skills which were strong enough to survive the deliberate colonial policy of suppression and imposed dependence on foreign products, were unfortunately deprived of the opportunity of being given effective scientific interpretation and development. Furthermore,

9

their processes could not be recorded in scientific language for posterity. It was inevitable, therefore, that traditional skills had to be preserved by the traditional method of passing them from craftsman to apprentice, or from father to son and so on through time.

The education provided for colonized peoples in Africa did little to stimulate local science. Early education in the colonies excluded instructions in scientific subjects. The first schools established in most of these countries were founded by Christian missionaries, whose main interest was to train African priests, who would assist European missionaries to spread the word of God amongst their brethren. Amazing as it may sound, what became the first Western University in the area was established in Sierra Leone in West Africa in 1827. It taught no science subjects. Although others followed some one hundred years later in Ghana, Nigeria, Uganda and elsewhere, in none of these universities were science courses introduced, until the middle of the twentieth century. This of course, was the time when the African's demand for self-rule reached its most aggressive stage. Then, the African's consciousness for improving his lot, had risen from the heat of resentment of his domination for decades by a foreign power. From that point onward, Middle Africa wanted progress, and that meant full understanding of the knowledge and practices, which were presumed to be responsible for the superior style and quality of living of the European.

Unfortunately, these goals, though understandable, were much too trivial and unprogressive. In addition, the instruments chosen in most countries for effecting the required scientific progress, were based on models developed by those very European nationals, whose countries had planned and executed the suppression and dehumanization of the African and the exploitation of his country. The result was, that those countries got what they wanted – science, but not science geared to the better understanding of the local environment and exploitation of its resources, rather, science which prepared students for life in advanced industrialized societies.

10

So, Middle Africa produced mostly the intellectual snob, whose knowledge was acquired for himself alone, so he could put himself on a high social rung from which he could speak down to his less favored countrymen. The Europeans, too, got what they devised; an education which would stimulate demand for Western manufacturers and so open endless commercial possibilities to the western manufacturer and merchant. Not until the beginning of the present decade did it become apparent to the nationalists in Africa, that the acquisition of Western Science was not by itself the end of the matter. It had to be digested, oriented and diffused into the society, until it became part of the mechanism for achieving a self-reliant economy.

The growth of science and technology activities in Middle Africa in the period following self-rule, took place because of political decisions to build up a strong science and technology infrastructure in the countries of the sub-region. The nineteen sixties and seventies, saw great strides being taken to expand science and technology activities. There was a determined effort to increase technological knowledge. Scientific and technological manpower was increased, mainly through training in local institutions, which themselves were multiplied and diversified to provide various levels of training. Industries were set up, many of which were modern and sophisticated, and produced consumer goods and certain classes of capital goods. Scientific and technological research was intensified to support the agricultural and mining sectors, to improve the building industry and to modernize the health services. In the process of building up these capabilities, excellent science and technology facilities emerged in some countries and quite a healthy crop of talented young scientists and engineers began to lead these fields of endeavour. Not all countries were able to rise to the challenges of training for the desired scientific transformation. Many stayed glued to the old pattern of education, exclusive of science, and have suffered the consequences of doing nothing to diversify education and training for their growing young population. Many countries in the vanguard of change have seen a quickened pace in

11

their development, both socially and economically. For some, however, this was maintained at great social and foreign exchange costs. Some resulted in failure. Furthermore, it was bringing many of the new nations of Middle Africa virtually to their knees in humble dependence upon foreign inputs into technological systems, for which there were no prospects of long term fixation within their societies.

It appears, however, that a new awareness of the problems of development is dawning and that more positive steps need to be taken to determine the role which Africa should play in the world's technological scene. Quite apart from this, attention is now directed, and happily so, to Africa's neglected indigenous technology. Three new demands are being made in this area by a concerned scientific community: the demand, firstly, for the adoption of scientific and technological systems which would relate with, invigorate and give direction to Africa's own existing indigenous technologies; secondly, the demand for the application of scientific principles in the creation of indigenous systems utilizing indigenous resources. The third demand is for devising methods to arouse the sensitivities of talented young Africans to the great prospect of bringing reputable scholarship to the search for traditional practices which have scientific and technological relevance to development.

All these demands constitute the challenges of the future; a future in which the scientists in Middle Africa must have one foot pushing back the frontiers of existing knowledge, and the other exploring the dark recesses of the continent's technological past with a view to utilizing the findings for modern development and the demands of modern living.

12

Chapter 2

Background to Sierra Leone's Higher Education

Perched on the West Coast of Africa between the Republics of Guinea and Liberia, is the picturesque land mass of the country called Sierra Leone. The capital, Freetown, is sited on a peninsula with an early history of Portuguese exploration [3]. The first group of explorers arrived in the country in 1492.

Freetown became a colony of Britain in 1808, following the settlement of the peninsula area by a mixed group of European philanthropists and black people of African descent [4]. British influence in the country extended beyond the peninsula in 1896, when large areas of the hinterland were annexed to the colony as a Protectorate to stave off French acquisition of the northern kingdoms. This arrangement enabled the colony administration to establish authority over the entire area.

Throughout its early history, the country was exposed to western education introduced by Christian missionaries who built schools and training centres in many parts of the country. In 1827, a college of higher education was established in Freetown on the coastal plains of the district of Fourah Bay. It became known as Fourah Bay College and was affiliated to Durham University in England in 1876, for degree-granting purposes. The first qualifications were awarded to Fourah Bay College students in 1879. The relationship with Durham continued until 1972 when the University of Sierra Leone Act was passed by the nation's Parliament. Thereafter, graduating students received University of Sierra Leone degrees. During the period of colonial rule, the country was acknowledged as the foremost centre for higher education in the sub-region.

13

Fourah Bay College building at its original site in Fourah Bay in the eastern part of Freetown.

Fourah Bay College attracted West African students aspiring to gain the best available higher education in the region. When Britain introduced constitutional changes, which would eventually lead to independence in 1961, it galvanized the people into action aimed at transforming the country into a united and prosperous land, with expanded opportunities to satisfy needs in all areas of human development. Particularly, the nation was determined to solidify the gains which had accumulated over a century and a half of

14

educational advancement. However, the years preceding independence brought their own challenges and Fourah Bay College had its own share of these. It offered mainly liberal arts education and was starved of funds for any diversification or expansion beyond certain prescribed curricula.

For a long time this situation threatened to delay progress in many sectors of development. Forward looking educationists had seen the threat and had been concerned about the weakness of the training then being offered at the college. They knew that the higher education system in the country had to be revitalized by providing facilities to undertake relevant training and research, as well as satisfy the nation's manpower needs. National manpower priorities had to be enforced by a well structured education policy. At Fourah Bay College, changes were being proposed that would entail diversification of course offerings at the college. These began to be introduced as the country gradually advanced towards independence. The first attempt to initiate diversification of curricula was made in 1954. Coming after one hundred and twenty-seven years of progress in providing higher education in the country, the move was considered daring. It involved the expansion of the college's curricula which then was almost entirely based on disciplines in the liberal arts and basic sciences, to include studies in engineering. The proposal for this expansion emanated from a visit to the college by a Commission appointed by the Governor in 1954 to make recommendations, inter alia, "on a long-term policy for Fourah Bay College". As a result of the findings of that Commission, degree courses in Science and diploma courses in Civil, Electrical and Mechanical Engineering were to be established in addition to the degree courses already established in Arts and Economic Studies. The commission's recommendations in respect of engineering were implemented in 1957, with one full-time lecturer and a handful of students, in a single department offering courses in the three main fields of engineering.

By this action, the first semi-professional courses were admitted into the family of academia. It was hoped that others would follow as the country slowly took responsibility for its own development. Surprisingly, it had to take another thirty years before the authorities at Fourah Bay College and the Government embarked on a course of action that would lead to the introduction of other professional courses; those of medicine and other health sciences. Even so, the further development of engineering as a discipline in its own rights at the college was obstructed at every critical stage of its progression to becoming a faculty. In later years, the attempt to introduce medicine and health sciences within the academic structure of the college became as controversial as the proposal in 1948 by the Colonial government to downgrade the status of the college to a polytechnic. While in the nineteen forties the college was united against the Colonial government's proposal, which was eventually withdrawn, it was bitterly divided over the issue of expansion of course offerings to include medicine.

The resistance to expansion of disciplines to include professional faculties was believed to emanate from conservative scholars, who felt that the trend would diminish the college's reputation as a liberal arts college. Yet, the college had earlier in 1928, through co-operation with the government of Sierra Leone, commenced a Normal Course for the training of teachers for the elementary schools of the Colony. The college had also endorsed the amalgamation of the Methodist Women's Teacher Training College with the College in 1945. The conflict of the new engineering programmes with long cherished academic traditions, impacted negatively on the momentum of progress towards a positive direction of change. The effect was to slow down growth of the developments that were initiated in 1954. It also discouraged the government from providing the increased funding levels necessary for this growth to take place. In a way, it prevented the rapid replacement of foreign experts in technical departments of government and harmed the country's capacity to be involved meaningfully in the appropriate choice and transfer of advanced technology.

Not surprisingly, the same conservative feathers that were ruffled at the thought of science and engineering intruding into the sanctuary of the humanities, were equally uneasy at the change of status of the college when its relationship with Durham ended in 1972. An act [5] of parliament had brought into existence the University of Sierra Leone. Many of the conservative individuals belonged to a college proud of its long academic tradition and particularly of its association with Durham University. They referred to themselves as "men and women of the Durham breed." Even discounting the unpleasantness of those who openly rejected the changes that were unfolding before their very eyes, the transformation of the small beginnings of engineering from a single struggling department to a faculty was a painful process. Every stage of it was fraught with obstacles, many of them deliberately planted to frustrate the progression from one stage of development to another. This book is devoted to that story.

Chapter 3

State of National Science and Technology in Sierra Leone at the dawn of Independence

At the dawn of independence, Sierra Leone was looking forward to improving its status in all sectors of human activity. It had missed science and technology developments that were taking place in Europe and elsewhere. It knew that entering the mainstream of this development would require a change in educational philosophy as well as the country's willingness to accept that change. This was a time when every citizen was bursting with pride at having a country with a new political status; prouder more so, for achieving that status peacefully. It was patently clear at the time, however, that all parts of the country would have to be brought into the independence age, and that that age should be one which ushered in improved standards of living, supported by the conveniences of modern technology. Measuring the new state against other nations, it could be seen that wearing the independence label did not automatically remove the underdeveloped state label, which was inherited from the country's colonial past. Muscular power predominantly drove the country's productive activities. Mechanized methods for undertaking these tasks were still beyond the financial means and the technical capability of most of the nation's workforce.

In most areas of the country the means of production had remained unchanged for generations. Craftsmanship in iron, gold, wood, and ivory, was limited to the production of household goods and implements for farming and warfare. These products were destined for the local market. Although these activities were supported by a strong raw material base industry, they did not benefit from skills advancement that normally comes from research followed by innovation. Traces of early indigenous technology had disappeared before they could be influenced or improved by modern science.

18

With the level of technology practised in 1961, it was impossible for local production of basic goods to rise higher in quality and quantity than it was, to meet the requirements of the growing population. The people, too, were becoming more diverse, with widely varying sophistication in taste.

The country remained largely forested. The denseness of the vegetation in some farming areas and the problems of weather and disease, had adversely affected the large-scale rearing of cattle and horses. In the absence of the plough therefore, farmers continued to employ manual methods for cultivation, in which the axe, the cutlass and the hoe featured as principle implements. Even as late as 1961, the growing of crops was subjected to a gradual adjustment of patterns and skills to provide food for large concentrations of the population. This selectivity was intended to establish crops, which were suited to the environment and whose yields satisfied the requirements of the community. Without chemicals and fertilizers, the systematized agricultural process of leaving cultivated land to lie idle for locally determined periods helped to enrich the soil after cultivation. For an expanding population, this process was unlikely to be always effective. Land availability might become scarce. Available land would therefore need to be utilized more frequently than tradition allowed. Experience in some farming districts was revealing that there have been periods of shortage, when reserve stocks from a previous harvest of the staple food crop were exhausted before harvesting of the new crop was due. It had even been worse in some areas, when old stocks were exhausted even while the new planting season was in progress. However, the absence of mechanization and the limited use of animals in the country to power production processes, affected agricultural production, as it did the production of locally made goods. Also, severe setbacks were being experienced in protecting high yields in certain types of crops, because of the absence of locally conducted and directed scientific research to reduce post-harvest losses and replace the slow manual method of crop harvesting.

In one skills area, weaving, good quality textiles were being produced. The traditions of dyeing and textile manufacture were continuing successfully and production of attractively dyed cloth was increasing. This skill seemed to have survived the competition from imported wax printed cotton cloth that gained popularity during the colonial period. Dyeing had a long history in the country, but extraction of dyes was carried out by a manual process which had not changed for generations; the industry's survival would require mechanization of the system to raise the level of production to a level that would enable it to start exporting gara cloths to markets overseas.

The loom was an important tool of local origin. Without a concerted effort at mechanizing the weaving process, this industry would gradually suffer the same fate as other traditional techniques which had vanished in the long march to independence. The same technical limitations existed in the practice of traditional medicine and in the construction industry. In the treatment of infectious and other diseases, herbal skills were widely used. These ancient skills required improvement in instrumentation to make them acceptable to the modern epidemiologist. It was expected that Science and Technology development in an independence age should in the future provide this transformation.

In construction, traditional methods continued to be employed largely in communities outside the main towns and villages for the construction of homes and accesses. Housing construction was carried out using mud and wattle, or sun-baked clay blocks. The floors were constructed from a mixture of mud and cow dung and the roofs from special grass or woven bamboo branches. The wattle was made up of bush sticks woven into a lattice. This was daubed with moist soil or clay and finished with evenly spread mud or clay mix. The method had been used for thousands of years. Durability was a problem as the walls had to be replaced every few years. Its sustainability as a cost-effective building material was an issue which required addressing. Without the involvement of appropriate technical knowledge, the cost advantage in using this type of building would disappear. In the capital city and provincial capital towns, the architectural forms of the early colonial period continued to be adopted, with a few notable exceptions seen in the construction of banks and other commercial buildings. Needs still existed for new school buildings and new hospitals. Also, there was need to expand recreational facilities in the country. The existing facilities were substandard for use in high quality competitive games and sports. Building standards had been well maintained in the construction of new facilities. The architects and engineers responsible for the design and construction of these and the grand colonial buildings, as well as the large and impressive government buildings, were foreign trained.

Over the years of colonial rule, however, skilled local construction workers had served the building industry well, constructing homes in towns and villages all over the country. In the city of Freetown some of these are of distinct architecture, traceable to the early period of resettlement in this part of the country. Their unique timber structure remained only as a monument to its past grandeur, as it was being rapidly replaced by buildings made of concrete, stone and building blocks. The most widely used building blocks were made from cement-stabilized sand or laterite gravel; no standards existed for its production and use. As a result, this new material was being used without technical specification and the quality of blocks made from it varied widely from the permissible to the unusable. Where imported materials were used in the higher end of the industry, these were expected to meet British standards. In many such cases the construction companies were British.

In general, the country's infrastructure, necessary for improving and sustaining the quality of life of its citizens, was basic in every sense of the word. What was inherited could only have been classed as poor. What was provided was limited to the urban areas. Citizens deserved better services and at independence were anticipating future improvements in every sector including, transportation, communications, water and power supply and public buildings. In the area of road transportation, most of the roads linking urban areas with rural areas were unpaved and dangerous to traverse. Only a few of these were taken across rivers by standard steel girder single lane bridges. Others, particularly those in outlying areas, had a part of the roads terminating at river banks. Vehicles and pedestrians then had to make the crossing by manually operated ferries, to join another part of the road on the other side of the river. Where they existed, the crossing at rivers was also facilitated by locally made bridges using palm logs as main beams and timber planks as riding surfaces. The main roads out of the capital city, Freetown, had been paved earlier. One led to the western peninsular villages and the other to the eastern suburbs, the provincial towns and villages. This eastern trunk road narrowed to a single paved lane barely 14 miles out of the city centre. Important provincial administrative centres and major agriculture and mining districts were served by this one road. Within them and beyond, mostly tracks dominated the countryside. Where these had been widened to carry vehicular traffic, they were rapidly ruined by heavy trucks which left the road surfaces riddled with pot holes, ridges, and corrugations.

Air transportation was developing slowly with one international airport and no national carrier. There were five local airports serving the provincial regions; one each at Hastings, Bo, Kenema, Kono and Bonthe. A deep-water quay had been constructed and was in use. For long distance internal travel, and for the transport of heavy goods and mail, use was made of the country's single line railway, which was put into service in March 1897. The width of the line was only 450 millimetres. It was gradually expanded between its launching and 1914 to serve destinations near and within reach of Wellington, Waterloo, Songo, Rotifunk, Bo, Baiima, Pendembu, Makeni and Kambia. Another line was built in 1903. This served the capital city, linking it with the residential district of Hill Station. It had a length of 8.9 km. The line was primarily intended to transport colonial administrators, who lived in this hillside area, to and from work in the city. The line was closed in 1929 as it was unable to compete with the growing popularity and convenience of the motor car. There had been improvements in the rolling stock over the years, but the size of the gauge had made significant development of the service impossible. With implicit faith in the railway, the British introduced diesel locomotives in 1950 and new freight wagons were acquired. The result of this new investment was to generate increased rail traffic, which grew steadily in the years of political advancement to independence. The Sierra Leone railway was further improved by an independence gift from Britain, of 45 new passenger coaches. By 1960, however, road traffic had increased and the limitations of the existing railway services were diverting passengers from rail travel to travel by road. There was a clamour for changes, and the population was looking to the new government for policies that would lead to the widening of the gauge and extension of the network to other economic centres, including the mineral rich districts.

The Post and Telephone Department had provided local telephone and postal services. External Telecommunication services were provided by the British company, 'Cable and Wireless'. Telephone connections to private buildings were limited. Radio broadcasts were via a re-diffusion service. The postal service was good and reliable in the city and district headquarters. There was a vibrant press with a rich history of leadership in the campaign for independence of the African sub-region. Typesetting was manual, but printing in the government printing department and the more popular local presses was by electrically driven presses. Lithographic printing methods were used in the production of newspapers and other high quality documents. Electrical power was generated by thermal power generators at two locations in Freetown, under the management of the Electricity Department. Power was generally available in the city, but distribution lines stopped well before the suburban populations were reached. They had to make do with oil lamps and candles. Water was also in short supply. The city of Freetown was supplied by a service reservoir at Tower Hill, situated just above the city's business district, a storage reservoir at Babadori in the village of Regent on the hills above the city of Freetown, and a storage dam in that same village. The available storage capacity was insufficient to satisfy the town's consumption needs. Shortages were frequent and citizens had to fetch water in buckets from fresh water streams flowing from the hills into the Freetown estuary. The situation was the same in provincial towns. The shortage of water and electrical power was hampering the transformation from desperate want, to civilized living.

The nation's standing in respect of its infrastructure, pointed to the urgent needs that had to be be satisfied in order to achieve significant improvements in the standards of living for all Sierra Leoneans. The investments needed in infrastructure would have to take place alongside investment in capacity building. Skilled manpower would be needed at all levels of these investments, for producing the hardware, that is, the machinery, developing the software for its operation, and operating the machinery itself. The availability of infrastructure professionals would be critical for the future development of the country. At independence, the country boasted of only fifteen (15) nationals who held technical qualifications. Three (3) of them were professional architects and twelve (12), professional engineers. It was evident that the country needed vast numbers of its citizens to enter the engineering fields. As the country moved into a more prosperous stage, it would need to deal with the safety of its infrastructural assets. Any unexpected natural or man-made event could constitute a threat to the stability of the nation. Floods, natural ground vibrations, large scale fires and other emergencies could cause safety concerns. The possibility of such emergencies required engineering skills either to avert them, or mitigate their effects on affected communities. The new government was aware of these urgent engineering manpower needs. In the years leading to the granting of independence, the pre-independence government had awarded scholarships to several young men and women to undertake further studies abroad in various areas of speciality including, Civil, Mechanical, Electrical and Mining Engineering. Until the country was able to train its own engineering specialists, these new engineers would be invaluable in the country's development.

The nation was entering a new phase of its history, depending for its development on investment capital derived from grants from Britain and the World Bank, on the one hand, and mineral licensing fees, royalties, and taxes from foreign companies, on the other. It was going forward with this range of investment potential, since it would be difficult to generate capital investment locally. Much of the country's internal assets could not be turned into capital, because many could not be traded at all, and others could only be traded within limited local circles. Technological growth was therefore going to depend on the political will of future governments, to give science and technology development the priority it deserved. In 1961, the leaders of the country knew the conditions under which the nation operated technologically. It had become their responsibility to implement measures to improve these conditions. The country had to move forward and those concerned about its future knew how they would like to see it advance. There was no "do nothing" option to contemplate; only the desire to join the planning on "how to get there". There was a general feeling among most patriotic Sierra Leoneans, that those who wanted to progress would move with the tide of expectations and those who remained indifferent to change, would be left behind.

Chapter 4

Fourah Bay College and its Environs

Over the years of its existence, Fourah Bay College had grown in reputation as a higher education centre in the region. Students from the sub-region were being admitted in increasing numbers, the fathers of some of whom had themselves been students there. It boasted of the achievements of its alumni; possibly one of the greatest of these at the time being Samuel Adjai Crowther (the first name in the College's Register in the year the College was founded), who became Bishop of the Niger and was later awarded an honorary Doctorate of Divinity by the University of Oxford. The college also counted among its former students, Prime Ministers, and Chief Justices in West Africa, and a host of professional men and women in all walks of life. Although it was founded by the Church Missionary Society (CMS), London, for the purpose of training Africans as schoolmasters, catechists and clergymen, it had moved on, following its affiliation to the University of Durham to enlarge its scope to allow for the admission of other students. Support for the college grew with the association of the Wesleyan Missionary Society (WMS) with the C.M.S in 1918 in the control and work of the College. It was respected for the effectiveness of its governing council, representative of both CMS and WMS Societies.

During critical periods of its development, it had faced and overcome threats to its survival. During the Second World War, it had survived the dislocation and disruption of its academic activities, when the British took over its original site in Freetown because of its strategic location on the coast. The government then adapted the building for use by the Admiralty. The threat of the war years was calmly overcome. The faculty, staff, and students were relocated forty miles away in temporary facilities in Mabang, in the south of the country. On its return from Mabang, the college had

26

been resettled on a site with only basic facilities. It was a former military encampment with an underground shelter. There was a general belief among students that the shelter led to a tunnel with an exit at a point in the east of the city. This was a myth that gave the site an importance beyond its commanding view of the city. A collection of single storey buildings located at various levels on this hilly terrain once provided all the accommodation available for classrooms and students residences, some of which were converted Nissen huts. Perhaps the only relief from the uninspiring infrastructure was the college's location, which somewhat compensated for various inadequacies. Overlooking the city of Freetown, it is still perched on a range of hills which rise from the city to Mount Aureol, 800 ft. above sea level and higher still to the Havelock Plateau, about 1,200 ft. above sea level, and commands splendid views of the city and harbour of Freetown, the Sierra Leone River, and the countryside stretching away to the mountains of Guinea.

Despite its meagre physical infrastructure, the college's popularity grew in the West African region; its role was progressively seen as crucial for the economic and social development of the country. The colonial government therefore became involved in its running and in 1948 threatened to downgrade it to a polytechnic. In May 1950, the government issued an ordinance establishing a new Council, representative of itself and all sections of the community, including the Missionary Societies. In 1959, the Teacher Training Department was removed to an independent college in temporary buildings at Tower Hill, within easy reach of the centre of Freetown. Later, it was moved to new premises in Goderich, in the western fringe of Freetown, and became the Milton Margai [6] Teachers College. An act of parliament passed in 2002 upgraded it to a polytechnic with a new name, Milton Margai College of Education and Technology, and an extended scope to include training in science and technology. Fourah Bay College then moved towards University College status. In January 1960, a Royal Charter was granted constituting Fourah Bay College as the University College of Sierra Leone.

With government becoming more involved with the college at council level, the academic character of the college began to change, and government priorities for the nation's development had to be taken seriously. Even so, obstacles to structural change and changes in academic course offerings were slowing down progress in the academic expansion of the college during the challenging years preceding independence. However, the pace of change grew a little faster when a first Sierra Leonean principal, Dr. Davidson Nicol [7] came into office in 1960. He had distinguished himself in the area of medical research and arrived with ideas which were to change the direction of development of the college after independence in 1961. Under his management, the college saw impressive changes to its physical and academic character from its earlier state. He continued the programme of renovation and reconstruction started under his predecessor, J. J. Grant, with grants from the Colonial Development and Welfare (CD&W) Fund. The programme of development included laboratories for the departments of Chemistry, Physics, Zoology and Botany; new buildings for Mathematics, Geography and Engineering, dining halls and halls of residence for men and women students, a student's union, 45 new staff houses, and carried out improvements to roads and services generally Also, the receipt of a gift from the Diamond Corporation of West Africa, then a principal exporter of the country's diamonds, made possible the establishment of a Department of Geology and erection of buildings for the department. In Dr. Nicol's grand plan, there were well laid out schemes for the complete redevelopment of the central area of the college which included a new library, Department of African Studies, Arts block, Economics block, Administration building, a building for the Education Department, and the erection of a Great Hall and Chapel. The construction of the last two never materialized in his time, nor did his ambition to establish courses that would eventually lead to the training of capable young people in the field of medicine. It fell on the shoulders of successive principals to accomplish these plans. Both Professor Harry Sawyerr and Professor Eldred Jones, tried to follow the grand plan drawn up during Dr. Davidson Nicol's term as principal.

28

By 1962, a recognizable pattern of development could be identified. New administrative and academic buildings dominated the landscape of the set of hills that constitute Mount Aureol, the name that has come to symbolize higher education in this part of the country and overseas. Rising uphill from Mount Aureol, a narrow road snakes around the new residential block for female students. This is the Lati Hyde Hall [8].

Start of Kortright hill climb. Lati Hyde hall is situated on the slopes on the right of the bend. On the near right is the wall of the reservoir serving the main campus and adjacent to it is the residence of the matron of Lati Hyde hall.

*The narrow hill climb from the main campus to staff residences
at Mount Aureol, Kortright.*

Half way up, to the left of the road, is the school built to provide
easy access to primary education for children of the College's staff,
most of whom were recruited from Britain. The first headmistress
of the school was Mrs. Oni Gabbidon, a highly-respected Sierra
Leonean educator. On the right, hidden behind tall flamboyant trees
are staff houses, some inherited from the military and renovated to
provide attractive homes for academic and senior administrative and
technical staff. These wooden frame houses with front verandas,
are discretely spaced to provide privacy; every space occupied by
flower beds and manicured lawns. The college's Plant and Gardens
Department had the responsibility of maintaining this garden
campus. At the top of this climb, the newer set of residential
bungalows spread out in silent unison, one white painted sand-
cement block house after another, with walls supporting gable
asbestos roofs. The risk to health of this material had not then been

30

acknowledged; so, protected by hardboard ceilings, occupants of these bungalows served out their terms without thought of any occurrence of health conditions that might affect them in future years. Beyond these residences, tall forest trees once lined the narrow gravel tract that leads to the villages of Leicester and Gloucester [9], their foliage blending with the distant greenery that adorns the slopes of Mt Sugar Loaf [10], the jewel of the Peninsula Mountains.

In a way, the introduction of engineering courses was responding to the need for trained personnel that would be required for the development of the country's physical infrastructure as well as its productive sector following the country's independence from Britain. However, the establishment of the new department, created in 1957 to run these courses, still had to face the suspicion and rivalry, that often permeated meetings of the academic board, whenever provision was to be made for its further progress. However, engineering continued to have the support of the college's administration. The single department was limited to providing instruction over a modest range of sub-professional courses. Even so, the popularity of these courses with employers in industry and prospective students grew, albeit under the shadow of liberal arts departments which regarded engineering training in their midst as inappropriate. Pure science departments, however enjoyed greater acceptability within the campus and their facilities, and courses expanded under Principal Nicol's plan to diversify the college's academic programmes. In time, those departments, too, became drafted into the opposing camp, intent on preventing any expansion of this single department of engineering, which then had the onerous task of training students in the three main disciplines of Civil, Mechanical, and Electrical Engineering. The transformation from that single department to a faculty was a painful process, every stage being fraught with obstacles. In the case of medicine, it was to be an even more painful path. It needed the establishment of a college, independent of Fourah Bay College, before that dream of Davidson Nicol's could be achieved.

In September 1962, I took up appointment in the engineering department as Acting Head. I was immediately drawn into the turbulent waters of academia a la Fourah Bay College, and made to take responsibility for steering the course of that progression. This was the time when the College was finding its way out of the funding difficulties in the fading years of colonialism. The national government which took over responsibility for the college from the CMS and WMS, found itself unable to support the aspirations of the college at the level needed for its successful operation. In spite of this, the college was making every effort to accommodate relevant expansion programmes within the cost envelope to which it was restricted. Every adjustment to satisfy relevant academic needs met with objections from older departments and faculties determined to maintain the level of funding for older courses. While government and college were dithering over prioritizing academic needs, all around the continent of Africa expansion was taking place in higher education, mainly in diverse fields of science and technology. English-speaking African countries, such as Nigeria, Uganda, Ghana, and Zambia, with institutions of higher education established after gaining political independence, were broadening their course options to include science and engineering. Their determined efforts at that time were predicated on the belief that it was time to progress beyond the known achievements of the African past and join the mainstream of technological development that was revolutionizing the world.

Leaders in these countries had become familiar with and proud of their heritage, thanks to the writings of African historians and anthropologists, which told of the continent's advanced civilizations and cultures dating back as far as the seventh century BC. These civilizations had cultures with distinct craft skills and architectural traditions. While such skills, notably in the production of wool, cotton and silk, were highly developed along iron works, textiles and gold and copper refining, all of these activities had failed to benefit from the industrial revolution which propelled Europe into industrialization and unprecedented economic growth in the 19th Century. The scientific and technological knowledge gap, as well as

32

the economic gap between Africa and the industrialized world, had since widened as trade barriers and conditions for the transfer of technological knowledge from the former European colonialists, to their former colonies, became insurmountable at every access point. Many of the new leaders of Africa were sensitive to their state of under-development and were anxious to propel themselves into the modern world. They were aware of the growth in importance of Africa as a strong raw material exporter while its appetite for imported capital and consumer goods increased to the detriment of its traditional science and technology.

The years of struggle for independence brought consciousness to many of that predicament. Nationalists[11] were outspoken about the nature of the education once prescribed for the colonized peoples of the region, and argued that it did little towards the development of local science. That education had excluded instruction in subjects which gave scientific information of any kind. Many leaders in most of the emerging nations believed that the situation had to be changed, and some were already doing just that in countries near and distant from Sierra Leone. Determined efforts were being made in these countries to increase technological knowledge. Technical manpower was being increased in training institutions, which themselves were multiplying in these countries and diversifying to cover most of the areas of expertise for which training had earlier been sought from foreign institutions. In Sierra Leone, pre-1960 planners had been unable the see the need of post-independence Sierra Leone, for a college that refocused its direction to give priority to areas of scholarship and research, that had the potential of making significant contributions to the economic prosperity of their nation. The country's university college had gained renown for excellence in the humanities and had stamped the college as the foremost institution of higher learning in West Africa, producing graduates of the highest quality in the arts and theology. This achievement, no doubt had blinded the planners' vision of the future.

In the years following the establishment of courses in engineering, more daring excursions were made into science and engineering, all amidst periodic onslaughts into their reputations as academic disciplines. At the college and in government circles, the introduction of agricultural sciences was being considered as an important development for a country with vast agricultural potential. In pursuing this initiative, the Sierra Leone government received support from USAID (the United States Agency for International Development), for the establishment of a degree granting college of agriculture and education, [12] in the southern town of Njala. In 1964, formal courses commenced following the conclusion of arrangements with the University of Illinois to provide necessary academic and managerial personnel and equipment. The government of Sierra Leone had then taken full responsibility for the development of higher education in the country. It saw the need for more institutions of higher learning in the country, outside the capital city and in areas targeted for rapid development. It was envisaged that the new college would develop as an independent entity without the limitations that could have been exercised within an enlarged Fourah Bay College. However, financial pressures from the older Fourah Bay College and the newly established Njala University College, forced the government to bring the two colleges under a central administration in an act of Parliament passed in 1967. That act created The University of Sierra Leone, transforming the two colleges into constituent colleges of the university and establishing two other constituent institutions, the Institute of Public Administration and Management, and the Institute of Education.

The new central administration of the new university soon found itself grappling with the same financial inadequacies as the two administrations it replaced. With competing demands for operational funds from other development sectors, the government's annual subvention to the university always fell short of the requirements of its budget. Therefore, the process of budget allocation between the colleges often became contentious and acrimonious. The spectre of two formerly independent institutions competing with each other for allocation of funds to run approved programmes was disconcerting. That funding rivalry often degenerated into hostility which extended to relationships between individual functionaries at the two colleges. Within colleges the distribution of funds to departments was equally controversial. At Fourah Bay College, it was funding for the development of the department of engineering between 1962 and 1967, that attracted the greatest opposition and sparked off bitter debates about academic programme priorities. This was a disturbing situation, in a country emerging from colonialism. As pressure on the college by government and the business community to introduce more relevant programmes began to mount, it became inevitable that a greater proportion of future investments would be directed to the establishment and strengthening of disciplines that included the new science and technology fields, which were in greater demand. Those demanding changes were also aware that in the end, the success of these disciplines would depend on the effectiveness of teaching and learning methods and the dedication of staff to the promotion of scholarship and innovative research.

In time, closer attention began to be given to critical assessment of cost effectiveness, product demand, impact on society and the economy, and quality and size of faculties and institutes. This meant that reallocation of investment in programmes, would become necessary at some stage and would culminate in priority re-grading in which the older faculties would come out worst in the process and, in some cases, even risk being phased out.

Chapter 5

The Early Days of Engineering as a Discipline at Fourah Bay College

Initiating Policy Change

The Commission, appointed by the Governor in 1954 to recommend a long-term policy for Fourah Bay College which then had three faculties, namely, Arts, Theology, and Economics, envisaged a phased development. It was to have courses in engineering taught alongside courses in science. Basic science courses were already being offered to students qualified for matriculation under the University of Durham's admission regulations and extended over five terms. While the recommendation in respect of science was to develop the existing basic science programmes to degree standard, the plan for engineering was to establish diploma courses, running concurrently with the basic science courses and covering the disciplines of Civil, Electrical and Mechanical Engineering. Under an arrangement with Durham University, engineering diploma students who attained a high level of pass in their final diploma year, were accepted into the engineering faculty at Kings College, Newcastle-upon-Tyne, then a college of Durham University, to continue their studies to degree level. The primary object of the diploma, however, remained the preparation of students for appointment as engineering assistants in Government service and in industry, where demand was growing for middle level technical manpower.

By 1960, the faculties which constituted the academic arm of the college had risen from three to six. These were Arts, Economic Studies, Theology, Education, Science, and Applied Science. The

36

departments in the faculty of Arts were Classics, English, History, Modern European and African Languages, African studies, and Philosophy. Courses provided within the faculty led to the degree of B.A. of the University of Durham. Candidates for this degree were also allowed to read Economics, Geography, Mathematics and Religious Knowledge, courses for which were provided in other faculties. There were Honours Schools in Mathematics and English. The departments in the Faculty of Economic Studies were Accounting, Economics, and Law. Courses provided within the faculty led to the degree of B.A. (Economic Studies), the Diploma in Economic Studies and the Diploma in Public Administration of the University of Durham. There was an Honours School of Economic Studies. There was just one department in the faculty of Theology. It provided courses in Religious Knowledge for the degree of B.A and a course for the Certificate in Biblical studies and for the post-graduate Diploma in Theology, both awarded by the University of Durham. In addition, non-graduate Ministerial Training Courses were provided. The Faculty of Education had a single department providing courses leading to the post-graduate Diploma in Education, and to the M.Ed. degree of the University of Durham. The Science Faculty consisted of the departments of Botany, Chemistry, Geography (and sub-department of Geology), Mathematics, Physics, and Zoology. Courses were provided within that faculty, leading to the degree of B.Sc. with Honours in Mathematics. There was a Department of Extra-Mural Studies, which was not within a faculty. As a service to the community, it provided extra-mural classes in Freetown, and had resident tutors in centres in the Provinces. They organized classes for the adult population in these centres. Short residential courses were also held in a wide range of disciplines in that department. The Faculty of Applied Science, like Education, had only one department in the faculty; that was the Department of Engineering.

The affiliation with the University of Durham enabled students pursuing degree courses in Arts, Theology, Science, Economic Studies, and the Post-graduate diploma in Education, to study and take their examinations at Fourah Bay College and, if successful, to have their degrees awarded by the University of Durham. Students, who successfully completed the basic science course, automatically qualified to undertake science-based degree programmes of Durham University. They were given the option to transfer to the United Kingdom to take those same programmes, or continue their completion at Fourah Bay College. The College only awarded its own Diploma in Engineering and Licence in Divinity.

The Faculty of Applied Science was given the responsibility for effecting the recommendations of the Governor's Commission as it applied to engineering studies at Fourah Bay College; that is, providing training to diploma level of Civil, Electrical and Mechanical Engineers, as a first step towards full professional engineering studies. The structure and content of these diploma courses were prepared in close collaboration with the Engineering Departments of the University of Durham. All courses covering the three branches of engineering were taught within a single department. Two buildings housed the department; one of them an old army guard room with an annex that once served as a garage. This building had been converted into offices for the Head of Department and his staff and a lecture theatre accommodating about 200 students. As if to isolate it from other departments, it was located downhill from the centre of the college campus.

Where it all started- the converted army guard room
This building became the main office and staff rooms of
the Department of Engineering.

The other building was a new two-storey building. It was constructed when the department was established and was designed to house the engineering laboratories and some classrooms. These were located opposite the Department of Zoology building, on a road leading to the Botany building, at the western edge of the college's botanical gardens. The building housing the engineering offices was only metres away from the engineering laboratories. The first head of department was Dr. Minwarin Prescod, who was provided on secondment from the Department of Civil Engineering at Kings College, Newcastle-upon-Tyne which, like Fourah Bay College, was then a college of the University of Durham. Kings College has since become the University of Newcastle-upon-Tyne. Under an arrangement with the University of Durham, responsibility for supervising the work of the department at Fourah

Bay College was assigned to the Civil Engineering Department at Kings College, then under the headship of Professor Fisher Cassie. He became the principal adviser to Fourah Bay College on the department's development.

The first group of engineering students was admitted in 1957. At that time, the diploma in engineering course was a blend of theoretical and practical training extending over three years. The first-year course consisted of basic science subjects taken in the science and mathematics departments, with students registered for the college's science programmes. Two other subjects, Engineering Drawing and Workshop Technology, were taken in the department's drawing office and workshop, respectively. The second year of studies consisted of full time industrial training given through attachment to industries with which the college had formalized a training programme. Students returned to college for their third and final year studies. They were given the option to choose subjects which would qualify them for the award of diplomas in any of the three engineering specialities. Packaged as it was, the diploma course was less noticeable than a well dressed academic degree course would have been, so it seemed unobtrusive to the academic purists. There was only one full year of engineering studies carried out at the college, and the department's activities were concentrated out of sight of the central campus. Albeit, with a staff of only three to cover the three specialities been offered, the department was able to turn out capable and competent products, the majority of whom were recruited into the government's technical services or absorbed into local industry. George Horton, who was among the first group of students admitted into the department, successfully passed his final diploma with distinction and was transferred to Kings College, Newcastle, to continue his studies for a degree in his preferred option, Civil Engineering,. Others qualifying with distinction followed him until 1965, when the department was restructured to undertake studies to degree level, under the authority of the University of Sierra Leone.

As the department developed plans for this restructuring, the attention of established departments and faculties became drawn to the impending threat to their dominance. It made the passage of proposals through the faculty and academic boards of the college for course changes stormy and their outcomes unpredictable. Nevertheless, it was recognized that the evolution of the department into a locally and internationally recognized centre of engineering excellence, could not take place within a structure that allowed only a single year for serious study of the engineering sciences. For the department to contribute more effectively to the overall needs of the nation and the industrial community which it was established to serve, it had to address other needs of industry and the nation, including the provision of professional and research engineers. This meant that it had to meet the call for relevance in its training and future research programmes, and that relevance ought not to be interpreted narrowly. It should encompass areas of knowledge and skills that would effect change in an area of the world that had been neglected in the march towards technological innovation. Courses should be such that they permitted students' minds to be stimulated through exposure to creative exercises and technical enquiry. New courses would, therefore, have to provide that exposure. With the attainment of self-rule, institutions such as Fourah Bay College were also expected to lead in bringing the benefits of modern technology to enhance the quality of traditional science and techniques. It required staff, committed to those ideals. At the diploma level, training was intended to follow a path that led to sub-professional employment. That objective should not be lost sight of while producing top class graduates in a mix of innovators and practitioners. In 1962, the department took steps to move gradually towards graduate training by restructuring the diploma programme and introducing new courses. The time allowed for learning and digesting the fundamentals of the engineering sciences was significantly increased.

That was when I arrived at Fourah Bay College. I had been preparing for this moment for over six months during which I received various communications relating to faculty activities and college development plans, all intended to keep me linked in a meaningful way with the college. A hot September morning saw me in the office of the Principal to report my arrival for duty as Acting Head of the Department of Engineering. The Principal's Office was on the top floor of a newly constructed three-storey Administrative Building. I announced myself to the secretary, a polite, fair-complexioned lady of medium height. I learnt her name later - Miss Samson. It went well with her memorable face.

The principal's office at Fourah Bay College.

The Engineering Department's secretary, Miss Jestina Nelson, had booked the appointment and I said politely,
"Good morning. I have an appointment to see the principal".
I sensed that Miss Samson was expecting me, but was surprised that she also seemed to recognize me. Obviously, she had seen the photograph I sent from the UK in response to a request from the

42

Principal who wanted it for a newspaper article on new staff appointments. Smart secretary!

"Welcome, Dr. Thomas," she said. "We are expecting you."

Miss Samson ran the Principal's Office with a messenger, a cleaner and two other secretaries, both of whom were hammering away at their manual typewriters.

"Thank you," I said.

"Could you please wait while I announce you?"

"Sure."

Five minutes later, she ushered me into the Principal's Office.

I remember the scene well. The Principal, Dr. Davidson Nicol, was seated at his desk, a long mahogany job, polished to a shade darker than the original hardwood. On the wall behind him were rows of photographs of his predecessors, showing the years during which they served:

1840-1858 Rev. Edward Jones, M.A.
1866-1870 Rev. Henry Jones Alcock, M.A.
1870-1882 Rev. Metcalfe Sunter, M.A.
1885-1889 Rev. Frank Nevill, M.A.
1890-1898 Rev. W.J. Humphrey, M.A.
1899-1902 Rev. E.H. Elwin, D.D. (later Bishop of Sierra Leone).
1902-1905 Rev. T. Rowan, M.A., B.D.
1911-1921 & 1925-1926 Rev. J. Denton, M.B.E., M.A., D.C.L.
1921-1923 Rev. F.B. Heiser, M.A.
1926-1936 Rev. J.L.C. Horstead, M.A. (later Bishop of Sierra Leone, and Archbishop of West Africa).
1937-1946 Rev. E.A.H. Roberts, M.A.
1947-1952 Rev. F.H. Hilliard, B.D., Ph.D.
1952-1955 F.R. Dain, M.A., Dip.Ed.
1955-1960 J.J. Grant, M.A., Ed.B.

These were the fourteen distinguished scholars who had made the college a citadel of learning of which the nation was proud. I was still gazing awestruck at the list when Dr. Davidson's voice came to me as if from a distance.

"Welcome to Fourah Bay. Please sit down. I am pleased that you have finally arrived. I hope you had a good trip. I am sure you will like it here."

I only half heard him, but I sat down in one of the arm chairs facing his desk and mumbled in what I'm sure was a preoccupied voice,

"Thank you, sir. I will like it here."

However, I quickly returned to the present when I heard him say, "Here are Dr. Majithia's handing over notes. Unfortunately, he could not wait to brief you personally as I had hoped."

Dr. Jay Majithia had been Acting Head of Department for a year, taking over from Dr Minwarin Prescod when he was withdrawn by Kings College, Newcastle, in October 1961. Dr. Prescod had served two two-year terms of secondment. A year before my formal appointment, I had been interviewed in Newcastle by Dr. Nicol and Professor Fisher Cassie[13] for the position of Head of Department which was due to be vacant when Dr Prescod's secondment to Fourah Bay College expired. As I could not take up the post at that time, it was agreed that, until I was available, a temporary arrangement would be made to fill the position . Majithia had been the stop-gap head, and I had been in correspondence with him ever since. He had kept me informed of all important matters relating to the management of the department during the year and I had hoped that he would stay and help me undertake the enormous task of developing a faculty from scratch. I was, therefore, disappointed that he had taken that decision to leave before I arrived to take over formally from him.

"Who else do we have in the department at the moment?" I asked.

"The Chief Technician, Mr Albert Smith. We expect a new staff member with electrical engineering speciality, Mr. Brian Nicol, to join us during the session."

I shifted in the chair, thinking: I might be grey by the time this Brian Nicol arrives and will have to run courses in Civil, Mechanical and

Electrical Engineering with only one Chief Technician to supervise the preparation of experiments for students, some of whom will be entering the final stages of their diploma.

Sensing my concern, Dr. Davidson Nicol said,

"We have been running the course with help from part-time lecturers recruited from industry."

Thank God, I said to myself, and aloud,

"I'd like to meet with them."

"I'll speak to the Dean of Applied Science to arrange it,"

A decisive man, Dr. Davidson Nicol, picked up his phone there and then and called the Dean to arrange the meeting. I was to see the Dean after my meeting with him.

Our conversation then switched to questions about my welfare, accommodation, transportation, medical and other social amenities available on the campus.

"Are you getting directions and advice on what we can do to make you comfortable here?"

"Yes, sir, I have already seen the Registrar, Bursar and Estate Officer. They have been most helpful," I replied.

He kindly permitted me to change the subject and I returned to departmental matters, wanting to know for how long the department would be confined to producing, what I then termed, 'ordinary level diploma engineers'. Dr. Davidson Nicol assured me that he would support any initiative to advance the current programme towards full professional courses. I registered this in my mind, and laid out beside it: Operation One: "Replace the one-year engineering programme with a three-year taught programme without affecting the industrial training component."

Dr. Davidson Nicol was to serve the college until 1968, during the last two years of which, he held the post concurrently with that of Vice Chancellor of the University of Sierra Leone, a development that brought together Fourah Bay College and the newly established Njala University College under a single administration. On leaving Fourah Bay College he served in two diplomatic

45

missions abroad, first as Sierra Leone's Ambassador to the U.N. 1969-71, and later as Sierra Leone's High Commissioner in London 1971-72. He left the diplomatic service in 1972 to take up the post of Executive Director, of the United Nations Institute for Training and Research, which post he held till 1983. During his term of office much progress was made in the development of science and engineering. On that day at his office, I exchanged views with a Principal who was genuine about his hopes for the department and the college. I had seen this in him during our meeting in London two years earlier, when he was searching for staff to help implement his expansion programme, and again in Newcastle-upon-Tyne a year later. Science and engineering were his promotion messages, but engineering had lagged the sciences since he took over the headship of the college. It had much ground to cover.

Science was then moving rapidly from merely symbolic existence to a substantive presence. It had gained importance as an academic discipline with the appointment of world renowned professors, such as Landour [14] in Chemistry, Bates[15] in Botany and Zulouf[16] in Mathematics. Quality research in these departments was beginning to be noticed as publications from them appeared with commendation in reputable scientific journals. Students from other parts of Africa were choosing Fourah Bay College as their preferred college of scientific studies. This had been the tradition in the case of the humanities, for over a century of the college's existence. Towards the end of the decade, however, the numbers of students from Nigeria and Ghana dwindled as those countries established their own universities; but they began to increase from other African countries, mostly from the southern states.

That day I left the Principal's office feeling happy with the reception I was accorded, and stepped out to the campus now throbbing with students just milling around or making their way to their classes. I had been to this campus, years before, but not as a resident. The first time was just after leaving school when I paid a visit to my cousin, Etta, who had entered the college to take an Arts degree. A year later, I was among a group of prospective engineering students taking introductory courses in Applied Heat and Engineering Drawing, to prepare them for studies overseas. The college had not then established engineering as a course of study. Those brief associations left no impression worth recalling nine years on. On this occasion, I was experiencing something different. The aura of the campus, the presence of older academics, rubbing shoulders with younger brains finding their feet in the labyrinth of academia, struck me profoundly. I noticed that registered students were still attending lectures in mandatory undergraduate gowns as before, and students' dining was taking place in dining halls under the gaze of Hall Wardens. This impressed me as the hallmark of stability, of a tradition apparently destined to continue for decades to come. Alas, by the mid-1980s that goblet of pristine heritage was crushed under the strain of financial pressure, brought on by the decline in funding for college programmes, and aggravated by growing student indiscipline. Fourah Bay College of the sixties epitomized the classic version of the academic campus, holding within its designated land boundary an integrated family of scholars, young and old.

I walked to the Dean's office, then situated in the Department of Mathematics, half way downhill towards the Engineering Department. Unless you were incapacitated or in a hurry for one reason or another, you walked up and down the hills of Mount Aureol from one office to another. The college's Grounds and Gardens department created the same garden environment around the central campus, as elsewhere on this unique site. Those walks were often mentally stimulating. Patches of greenery and the colours from flowering trees, relieved the monotony of the dark grey rock outcrops on the mountain slopes rising above the well of the central campus, and the blandness of the plain white façade of department buildings. I was going to discuss not just the staffing problems of the department, but the blueprint of Operation One that I had registered in my head. I did. The Dean was receptive.
"Let us see a plan for the changes you propose" he said as we parted.

47

One of the Department's buildings set behind towering trees.

Two weeks later, I had a plan to discuss with the Dean. Another week passed, before he was satisfied that he had a draft he could put with confidence before the Faculty of Applied Science. A copy of the draft proposal was submitted to the Principal, who endorsed it. A start for change had been made.

Planning Changes to Old Courses

The plan to extend the time spent on engineering studies at the college, made provision for some engineering studies to be introduced in the first year of study. Engineering concepts and principles would be incorporated in a new course titled, 'Descriptive Engineering'. During my university training in Scotland, I had admired this idea of introducing freshmen to the discipline before they were led deeply into it. My proposal for changes included replicating this model at Fourah Bay College. It would be taught in

48

addition to the basic sciences and mathematics. A three-month industrial attachment would complete the first-year programme. Before the proposed changes, students spent their second year, out of the department in industry. This period would be reduced to three months to allow for more engineering studies and laboratory work to be undertaken within the department. The third year would remain unaltered, but a report on specific projects carried out under supervision during their second year's industrial attachment would be required from students, and would be assessed as a subject in the final examination for the award of the diploma. There was more to the plan. It also included recruitment of more academic and technical staff, provision of workshop machinery and laboratory equipment, and improvement to the department's library, which I had set up on my arrival with books and donations from friends and former workmates in the United Kingdom (UK). The plan, if implemented, would be the staging post for the launching of degree courses.

For the training envisaged, access to good books was essential. Before my arrival in the department, standard engineering text books were not available in the main library for students' use. The library collection then catered primarily for the disciplines of the humanities. The engineering collection was small and somewhat unrelated to the level of the diploma courses offered by the Engineering Department. With a short course of the kind run by the department, I deemed it unreasonable for students to be asked to purchase books which were well beyond the range of their syllabi. The book scheme I had launched in the UK, met that need in providing books to which students could refer within the department. A good supporting library was a fundamental requirement of any programme for the transformation of the department, to academic credibility. I had taken over the spacious corridor of the department offices to set up the library. The front of the building faced the road. The windows on that side were small and narrow and set high above floor level. Thick metal bars ran across them, confirming the rumour that this was once a prison. I tried to create a scholarly atmosphere in the corridor of the building with a few reading desks and tall bookshelves, tidily stacked with gift books, reaching the ceiling, and covering much of the wall space left by the windows. On the other side of the corridor were staff rooms, one of which was reserved for the Head of Department. The secretary to the department became the department's honorary librarian. She used to sit in a corner of the entrance hall, facing the road. When I took office, I moved her to a space adjacent to the Head of Department's office and had a door fitted to give her the privacy a confidential secretary's office would require.

The Dean took the proposal for improvement of the quality of the engineering courses to the Board of the Faculty of Pure and Applied Science at its first meeting of the session. Membership of the board included representatives of the department of mathematics and the science departments, where engineering students spent their first year of study taking courses in chemistry and physics. It was on a Friday afternoon; members had arrived from their various departments and taken their seats in a classroom in the Mathematics department. Accompanying me and representing the Department of Engineering were Mr. Brimshire Akabi-Davies and Mr. Hero, two of the part-time lecturers with whom I had prepared the plan. Notice for the meeting and board papers had been circulated a week earlier, including our department's proposals. Since the document was no longer a secret, its contents had been widely discussed on campus by members of the board and aspects of the plan had already sparked opposition in many quarters.

The Chairman called the meeting to order, obtained confirmation of the agenda and proceeded to conduct business as itemized in the agenda. Somewhere in the middle of the proceedings, he invited discussion on the restructuring paper from the Engineering Department which I had presented. Tension rose in the engineering camp as speaker after speaker, who took the floor after me, made the case for rejection of the proposal.
"It is premature to modify a course so soon after it has been launched with fanfare by this college," proclaimed a representative

50

of the Physics Department. "And the college cannot afford it," he went on.

Those words almost killed the spirit of optimism with which the engineering group had arrived, for we knew he was speaking the minds of many in the room. Someone seated behind me whispered in my ear, "You can't get anything through this board with Physics against it."

A barrage of criticism from other board members followed this outburst, one even questioning the usefulness of a revised course to industry.

"This change is too precipitous," he declared, "and I believe that it has been made without seriously studying the existing programme, and taking the time to assess its value to industry, where products of the programme would have to seek employment."

Doubts about clearing this obstacle to the introduction of the courses increased among our representatives until the Chairman intervened to explain that the proposal had been carefully thought through, and that he and the Principal had given it their blessing. I still asked myself whether, with all this opposition it would ever be possible for this proposal to pass this board. But as the Chairman continued to speak, I could see in his face the potential for that possibility. He laid out the plan again, pointing out that it was the quality of the training that was the focus of the changes. Significant improvement to the present course would be welcomed by industry and would give students the excitement of exposure to deeper knowledge and a greater understanding of the hardware they might be required to operate in their industrial practice. "I urge you to approve this proposal," he said in conclusion.

The majority listened, but not enough for the board to pass the plan with a comfortable majority. I foresaw problems down the road, when, as it grew, the department would have to return with fresh development plans. However, passing that first proposal was all that mattered then. In keeping with academic board rules, a year's notice was issued for the introduction of the new programme. A higher quality diploma in engineering course, with enhanced academic status, commenced in earnest in October the following year.

The 1962-63 academic session was devoted to planning for introduction of the new courses, while the old courses were taught throughout the session to continuing students. Throughout the first and much of the second term, I was the only full-time lecturer at the department. I found myself teaching subjects in mechanical and electrical engineering that I had taken in my second year at university, in addition to subjects in civil engineering to final year diploma students. Towards the end of the second term, approval was given to recruit more staff. Brian Nicol was appointed lecturer in Electrical Engineering and Samuel Burney-Nicol, lecturer in Mechanical Engineering. Brian Nicol had taken his degree from a British university, but Samuel Burney-Nicol had studied at a German University, where the engineering course was structured to transform ambitious engineering freshmen into complete professionals by graduation. Burney-Nicol therefore proved to be an asset to the department during the initial years of developing new courses. His commitment to the quality of training the department had prescribed, was an inspiration to those of us who worked with him and particularly, to the part-time lecturers whose laboratory assignments for students he vetted and supervised with Germanic thoroughness. With three full-time lecturers, confidence grew in the department's ability to run the improved courses.

Lectures started at 8 a.m. I often walked to classes from Kortright, a plateau beyond the hilltop of Mount Aureol where I had been allocated a one-bedroom bungalow. Sir Cornelius Hendricksen Kortright, after whom this area of the campus was named, was Governor of Sierra Leone from 1875 to 1877. My bungalow was on the right side of the road leading to the villages bordering the college. With their stunning views, houses on that side were hotly contested for whenever they fell vacant, so I considered myself

52

lucky. Lecturers who lived at Kortright regarded themselves as belonging to a community with common interests and values, so newcomers soon became drawn into a close fellowship in which barriers of rank or nationality, perceived or real, were absent. The close fellowship among residents made this upper territory of the campus more attractive to many staff members than its lower parts where residences were dispersed awkwardly among faculty buildings, the Administrative Building, the college bookshop and the theatre, named after Mary Kingsley, a famous British explorer. Her expeditions and writings had revealed much of what was still unknown about Africa in the nineteenth century. The college bookshop, which was annexed to the theatre, served both staff and students. It was the most popular bookshop in the city since it also stocked books of general interest and music albums unavailable elsewhere.

.I enjoyed those early morning walks to my regular 8 a.m. classes. I walked back for lunch at 1.00 p.m. and returned to supervise laboratory classes which started at 2.00 p.m. The routine was the same for science based courses. Lecturers in the Humanities and Social Sciences, however, had a different routine which they proudly referred to as civilized schedules, saying,
"We leave ourselves more time to think than to scribble formulae on giant blackboards."

The main road through the residential area at Kortright with staff housing behind well tendered trees.

Row of staff houses behind lush front gardens at Kortright.

Bookshop and part of the Mary Kingsley theatre seen behind trimmed hedges.

In 1962, we were taking up the challenge to upgrade academically and physically, the smallest department in the college in terms of staff and student numbers. It was also the only department in the smallest faculty - Applied Science, a fact that soon caused controversy, the question being whether the faculty should remain in its present form. It might seem understandable that there should have been opposition to continuing to fund a faculty with just one department, at a level out of proportion to its size. The college record of student population for the 1961-62 session grouped the numbers for the Science and Applied Science faculties together which gave the combined number in these faculties as 30% of the total student population. The contribution of the Department of Engineering to that group was such a small fraction of that percentage that other faculties began to question the justification for having a separate faculty to regulate the affairs of the Engineering Department.

The problems associated with the revision of the course structure which I had proposed continued to mount. Accommodation and equipment were inadequate. More staff than had been recruited so far, was needed to cover the course options to be offered the following session. Positioned in the midst of these problems, I had only one way to go; that was to the Principal. Only he could find a way within the government's triennial grant to the college and the overseas assistance it received occasionally, to ensure that the department would be ready for the launch of the new courses in October 1963. A year and a half after independence, the county was still receiving goodwill visits and offers of help from friendly countries and international organizations, many of these showing an interest in assisting with education. On account of its long history, Fourah Bay College often received foremost attention. On the day, our secretary called the Principal's office to make an appointment for me to see him, she received information from Miss Samson, that the Principal would be receiving visitors to the college from Britain that day, and that he would be showing them round the campus. The Engineering Department was on the list of places to be visited. I called Miss Samson myself to check whether she could squeeze me in after the visit, as the matter I wanted to raise with Principal required his urgent intervention. Since the Principal would be busy all week with visitors, she could only give me an appointment for the following week. However, I had been thrilled by the news of the planned visit to the department. I passed the information to the rest of the staff in a memo that also summoned them to a meeting, to plan our strategy for what I thought was an ideal opportunity to show what we had, and highlight what we didn't and needed badly.

When the team arrived, we were ready to play our various parts. After a brief all-round introduction, I described the current training programme and the improvements we hoped to introduce in the next session, if everything went according to the proposed plan. We then led them first to the departmental library, the cramped space into which students had to file after lectures, to look up works to which they had been referred. Next, we moved into the little laboratory beyond the library space where students carried out tests to demonstrate some basic principles of mechanics and determine the strength of various engineering materials using simple portable equipment. As far as civil engineering was concerned, not more could be shown of laboratory facilities except a soil-testing laboratory with basic equipment to test soils, as well as properties of other building materials. This laboratory was located at the rear end of the top floor of the new building. Next to it, was the Drawing Office, equipped with drawing tables. Students brought their own drawing boards and drawing sets to classes. We showed the visitors both facilities, which had little to impress, compared to others they must had seen around the world. We also showed them the rest of the top floor which was equipped mainly with desk-top electrical engineering testing machines. The line-up of equipment was impressive; many standard electrical and electronics experiments could satisfactorily be conducted in this laboratory.

The ground floor of this building was more conveniently reached from the road, which ran between the building and the Zoology building. We entered this floor through a wide garage-type door that opened vertically with chains. It was through this door that most of the machines in the top and ground floors were offloaded. This floor accommodated the mechanical engineering laboratory. It contained some internal combustion engines, rigged to conduct experiments on many operational and performance indicators, and a medium-sized universal testing machine. The floor looked bare. Here and there were cut-off models of machines on stands. On the walls were displayed, pictures of plants and machines, with their parts appropriately labelled to assist students with their identification. Throughout the tour, my staff and I did our best, when describing what we had as training facilities. We demonstrated that we had to work with less than was needed to train engineers for the present and future needs of the country. As the visitors were about to leave this laboratory, I said, in the hearing of the principal, that the department had compiled a list of urgent requirements, which would be sent to the Principal's Office early the following week. I glanced in his direction; he was chatting with the British Council Representative who was with the visiting team.

As we walked back to the department's office for them to sign the visitors' book, Mr. Smith, the Chief Technician reminded us that we had not yet visited the workshop. He led us to a building, which was once a garage, but had since been slightly extended to accommodate two rows of light machines. The machines which looked new and well kept, were unusually quiet that afternoon as the junior technicians stood to one side to allow the visitors room to inspect the collection.

"How old is the workshop?" I recollect one of the visitors asking Smith.

"We set it up two years ago," Smith smiled, remembering what a wreck it had been before that part of the college was handed over to the department. He explained it used to be a repair bay for vehicles with unwanted vehicle parts and pieces of scrap metal filling whatever space vehicles under repair did not occupy. He pointed out the department's prized acquisition - an industrial lathe, and moved the visitors towards it to describe some of its features and demonstrate its use. Smith had done a good job with this rehabilitation, and I was happy to have him on board for the work that lay ahead. Our small workshop had already attracted the attention of the Marine Department and other metal works establishments in the city as a reliable and efficient centre for lathe work and was receiving commissions for producing machine spare parts.

When I saw the principal a week later, he had seen the submission I had forwarded through the Dean and was ready to discuss the contents of the document. He agreed with some of the items of need - more staff and more laboratory equipment. These he was convinced were vital to the running of the new programme in the 1963-64 academic session. He also supported the request for more professional machines for students and staff so they could fabricate material within the department for conducting experiments. We had included other items in the proposals, such as new accommodation for civil and mechanical engineering laboratories and a student's workshop dedicated entirely to training in workshop practice. These were not considered urgent.

I came from the Principal's office with instructions to prepare a formal request for equipment assistance to the Department of Engineering, which he could submit to overseas institutions that had expressed interest in helping him continue with the college's expansion plans. I had the satisfaction of knowing that I had at least justified most of my proposals, particularly for increasing the academic staff for the coming session. I was confident that I could include this increase in my proposal to the college's budget allocation committee, with high hopes for its approval.

The preparation of the equipment proposal was tricky. Apart from the normal generalities of project location, statement of purpose of the assistance, and history of engineering education at the college, the request had to include a detailed list of equipment required. Since there was no certainty of the source which the Principal would tap for assistance, brand name and country of origin had to be omitted, or a name 'or similar', added to quoted brands. But a project cost was required for the request to be given serious consideration. The Crown Agents of London were the exclusive suppliers of the college's educational materials, so there were catalogues of scientific and engineering laboratory equipment produced by British manufacturers available for consultation. The department submitted two schedules of equipment; one with brand names and cost obtained from these catalogues, and the other with only names, leaving out cost. We then waited for the kind hand of a donor to deliver a favourable response, for this equipment was vital to the implementation of the new Diploma in Engineering course.

Chapter 6

Implementing the new Diploma in Engineering Courses

Overcoming initial challenges

In March 1963, I was nearing the end of my first session at the college and feeling concerned about the rumblings on campus about the merger of the faculty of Applied Science with the faculty of Science. However, the proposal to merge these two faculties was not put before the Academic Board and Council of the college until the end of that month. It passed both bodies. It was a merger that was expected, considering the jabs of criticism that had been thrown at the single department faculty of Applied Science. By that merger, the engineering department came under the supervision of a newly constituted faculty of Pure and Applied Sciences, and so became open to the scrutiny of a larger number of board members who would be drawn from all departments of the new faculty. There were known critics of the department's plans to move to a higher level of training than was being given at the time, and more of these critics would be on the new board than in the one it was to replace. We realized in the department that it was going to be more difficult to pass any further upgrading proposals. We had to await these challenges. There was a long way to go to raise the standard of the college's engineering courses higher than the level of the new diploma for which new students would be admitted the following October. However, we believed that having moved some way towards our goal, we should embrace what we had gained and depend on impeccable performance to prove that we were capable of managing greater responsibilities and resources.

60

As fate would have it, besides being a member of the Faculty of Pure and Applied Sciences, I was, by virtue of my position as Acting Head of the Engineering Department, given the privilege and opportunity to represent my department's interest in the College Council. Other heads of departments in Council were my seniors in age, as well as academic achievements. They were running departments many times larger than mine, and each enjoyed an unchallenged reputation. While I sat in their midst, I felt an urge to close the academic gap between our department and theirs. I knew this would take years to achieve but was determined to use my seat in this forum, to garner support for our plans and aspirations. I cannot recount the number of times I received encouragement and advice from the small core of Sierra Leonean professors, who wanted to see the department grow and flourish; among them were Harry Sawyerr[17] of the Department of Theology, Arthur T. Porter[18] of the Department of History, Eldred Jones[19] of the Department of English, and Edward Blyden III[120] of the Department of African Studies. On the other hand, some of the younger academics were unable to support the bold steps being taken to diversify the college's training programmes, looking upon them as a waste of scarce resources.

Protests of a different kind were taking place on campus, with young lecturers demanding change to the college's dress code for lecturers. When they failed to overturn years of conformity with tradition, they demonstrated their frustration by mounting silent protests, including striding to lectures in shorts and flip flops, while keeping their gowns on their backs. They still had to put on ties to see the Principal and, in some cases, to see the Dean. Fourah Bay had its rules and they had been the anchor that sustained it.

Undeterred by these developments, the department continued to run the old courses, and devote time to the pursuit of the other essential elements of the college's mission; research and service to the community. Already, we were providing valuable workshop and materials testing services to local industry. In order to improve these services, the department set up an advisory services unit, giving it a broader scope of operation, which included professional engineering advice to local manufacturing and construction companies. Within a short period, it had established a reputation as a technical support centre for local engineering problems, especially those connected with materials and systems behaviour under tropical conditions. And we earned money for our services, all of which went into college's coffers. Our academic research activities were also proving to be a vital complement to our materials testing services. All the staff in the department had been allocated research grants on assumption of duty, as was the practice before 1980, when all grants were awarded on competitive basis. Starting with our small grants, we started investigating a number of local problems that needed serious study and most of our research findings and formulations found successful application in work done by practising engineers and industries. Some solicited help from the department's advisory unit. Though pursuit of our research interests was intense, we realized that our academic advancement in the college must go hand in hand with our promotion of the development of the department itself.

I had chosen to work on the properties of local building materials, although my earlier research interests were in the areas of plain, reinforced and prestressed concrete. At that time, I had a joint paper on shear stress with my former professor at Leeds University awaiting publication in the journal "Civil Engineering and Public Works Review"[21]. "There was no point continuing working in areas for which there would be little or no resources or facilities to support them", I tried to console myself. My administrative and teaching duties occupied much of my normal working hours. Therefore, to be able to meet my research targets, I often stayed in the department till the early hours of the morning, reviewing research results and preparing papers for publication. I relied enormously on the department's technicians for the conduct of experiments and on my secretary, Miss Nelson (now Mrs Carter), for typing my manuscripts. By the end of the academic session, I had research papers ready for publication in academic and technical journals. Some of these were also sent out in response to calls for papers to be delivered at technical conferences in Africa and elsewhere [22].

Annual examinations were drawing near for first and third year students, who were on campus. Second year students were spending the year in industry. That year the department had placed students on attachment for industrial training with local industries, such as The Aureol Tobacco Company Limited, The Sierra Leone Post and Telecommunications Department, The Sierra Leone Construction Company Limited, The Sierra Leone Petroleum Refinery Company Limited and The Palm Kernel Oil Mills, companies with which the department had standing arrangements. With more students expected to be deployed when the new diploma commenced, the department needed more industrial concerns to join the scheme. Throughout the Easter term, approaches were made to a number of potential participants. By the time the college closed for the long vacation, Sierra Leone Breweries Limited, British Petroleum Limited and the Sierra Leone Broadcasting Service had all joined the scheme. At the same time, as normal classes and preparations for examinations continued, the department was feverishly preparing for the changes to be implemented in the new session. We set up committees to draw up new curricula, reorganized existing laboratories to accommodate new equipment, and even re-examined previously allocated space to squeeze in offices for additional staff.

Towards the end of the academic year, the department received information on its budget allocation and staff increases approved for the coming session. Three new staff positions were created, more money was provided for hiring part-time staff and a small amount included for building maintenance and purchasing equipment. Fired up by that news, we set in motion the procurement process, engaging the Finance Office in discussions about ways to fast track the process. Without news of the fate of our request to donors, we were grateful for the funds provided in the regular budget and urged the Finance Officer to start placing orders for equipment and materials which they could cover. We were determined that the absence of donor assistance would not divert us from pursuing our goals.

Once examinations were over, we were able to deal with such matters as preparation of the department's annual report, time-tabling, preparation of students' booklists and supporting materials for each year of the new course. I worked on the annual report, receiving inputs from other members of staff. Mr Brian Nicol was put in charge of time-tabling and associated matters. Taking on that task was problematic. Science departments were reluctant to reduce their contact hours for first year engineering students to make room for the inclusion of two new engineering courses, Descriptive Engineering and Workshop Technology. The departments had to be persuaded that it would be unwise to increase the contact hours of these students beyond the load they currently carried taking lectures in the basic sciences. Finally, agreement was reached on a level of reduction that allowed the engineering department to allocate time amounting to three hours per week to each of the new courses. That problem overcome, Brian Nicol was confronted with another one involving the mathematics syllabus for second year engineering students; they needed a lecturer for certain topics which were prerequisites for taking final year electrical engineering courses. These courses, Brian Nicol found out, were not normally taught to Preliminary Year students reading mathematics as a main degree subject for a pure science degree. The mathematics department insisted that the department could only fit our second-year engineering students into existing Intermediate Year mathematics classes, even after appeals were made to the department's head at the time, to accommodate our mathematics requirement.

At that time, Fourah Bay College operated under the same academic term dates and names as Durham University - Michaelmas Epiphany and Easter terms, in keeping with the religious heritage of that university. Many other British Universities followed that tradition. The first term ran from October to December, the second from January to March and the third from April to June.

The new diploma was planned to fit into college term dates and course years adopted by departments operating under Durham conditions. Our second-year course became the Intermediate Year in keeping with college designation. There would be no equivalent of the Durham Qualifying year or pre-final, as students would take their final diploma examination in their third year at college. The difficulties with mathematics were overcome by having some topics relevant, particularly to electrical engineering students, taught by a lecturer within the department. Space remained a concern. This was going to be critical in programming classes. With the help of the Maintenance Officer, Mr. Richards, and the Estate Officer, Mr. Frank Fraser, a staff office and a classroom were created from the covered pavement at the back of the secretary's office. In the new building, another staff office and classroom were set up using hard board partitions. All were ready for use against the start of the new session.

Annual Academic Standards review at the University of Durham

In the period between July and September most senior academic staff of the college, would leave the campus on holiday. Their contracts entitled them to paid leave with passages paid for them and their families to the United Kingdom or similar destination. Staff with responsibility for marking Durham examination papers, spent some of this time in Durham and Newcastle, vetting marked scripts and attending examiners' meetings. Like other heads of departments, I left Sierra Leone to attend the engineering department's examiners' meeting in the Civil Engineering Department at Kings College, Newcastle-upon-Tyne. Mr. Burney-Nicol acted as Head of Department in my absence. The meeting was held in the morning. Afterwards, I spent some time with Dr. Prescod who had invited me for a chat at his office. He was keen to learn about the progress the department had made since his departure. I briefed him on the structure and content of the new diploma, and he wished us well, enquiring what help he could give.

"There's our departmental library project," I suggested.

It was all that came to my mind, knowing that his department was already helping the college in other areas. He had some text books he could give, he said. I promised to collect them later, thinking that Mrs. Carter, our librarian, would be pleased. We had already lost some of our stock to students who deliberately or inadvertently took books away in breach of departmental rules.

The following day I had a meeting with Professor Fisher Cassie and discussed the new diploma, a draft of which we had sent him, and the way forward to the establishment of degree courses. He thought the new course looked very much like the higher diploma in the United Kingdom and should be well received both locally and internationally. I was happy that we had managed to pitch the diploma at a level from which it could comfortably rise to degree level, without dismembering the framework of the diploma. I encouraged the professor to send an official review of the programme to the college authorities, as that would help the department to counter any opposition to further development of engineering courses. Cassie had a department that was one of six, in a faculty of engineering. It was expanding rapidly, attracting students from around the world, who were anxious to earn engineering qualifications from one of the leading centres of learning in Britain. Support for the work of the Newcastle faculty was continuously received from industry and the government. Fourah Bay College had moved much too slowly throughout the period of colonial administration and needed to make faster progress if it was to become a key player in the country's development. At the same time, a high level of training in engineering would re-establish its place as a leading centre of learning in West Africa. Being in a progressive university setting forced me to reflect on the difficulties of bringing about change in Sierra Leone. It made me sad to think that there were citizens who, obsessed with the past, could not envisage the college playing a leading role in national development, particularly in the training of engineers. Those of us managing the fledgling engineering department considered it our duty to work towards achieving that goal.

Following the Newcastle meetings, I visited the engineering faculty in Leeds, where I had friends who knew of the challenges I faced at Fourah Bay College and had supported my book scheme. I had been receiving advice, particularly from Professor R. H. Evans[23], a remarkable man, outstanding in his field but approachable and helpful. He had been my supervisor while I was a research student in his department. I discussed with him the progress we were making and sought assistance with teaching materials and spare equipment. He sat on several editorial boards of publishing companies and agreed to send the department more engineering textbooks from his collection of publishers' advance copies. Before I left his office, he had also called in his Chief Technician to search his workshop and laboratories for any spare portable testing rigs and other test kits which still had some useful life and report back to him. I was certain that if there were pieces of equipment of any significance found during his Chief Technician's search, he would have them sent to our department before long.

Two weeks before I was due to return to the department, I made a study tour of some British universities. The visits were organized by the British Council, whom the Principal had approached for assistance. I visited Loughborough, Southampton and Wales universities, my ears and eyes opened to record examples of best practice that would serve me in good stead on my return to my own department at Mount Aureol. I arrived back at Fourah Bay college to find that more students had qualified for the new courses than could be admitted because of the limits set by the science departments for first year admissions to their courses. That was a problem we had foreseen as the course had been given much publicity during the year. Apart from the usual notices published in the newspapers inviting application for admission to the various courses available at the college, Mr Burney-Nicol and I had visited a number of secondary schools in Freetown on the invitation of their principals to talk to fifth and sixth form pupils about careers in engineering and the opportunities for studying the discipline at

Fourah Bay College. These talks generated great interest among the pupils and may have been the reason for the more than normal volume of applicants intending to study engineering. The problem of over-subscription was one we were happy to deal with, for it gave us the opportunity to admit the best qualified students and start a change in admissions preferences that continued into succeeding years.

The worst of the rainy season was over, and the college was preparing to usher in the first term of the 1963-64 sessions. Activities at Mount Aureol prior to the start of term were always chaotic. Old staff members were returning to base; new staff finding their feet, clogged the offices of the Registrar, Mr. Manilius Garber, a distinguished lawyer, and administrator, and those of the Finance Department, then under the leadership of a seasoned accountant, Mr George Hamilton. Many demanded immediate solutions to their problems, the main ones usually connected with housing. Junior lecturers were often unhappy with their first housing allocations and tried to change them as they gained seniority. Some staff recruited from Britain, sought clarification on some of the conditions in their FSSU policies [24], while others sought college sponsorship for car loans or bridging loans to offset expenses incurred in relocating to Sierra Leone from their previous countries of abode. On assuming office, the Principal had secured the services of the best talents he could find to join him, so the college had a large number of expatriate lecturers and professors at the time. They and their Sierra Leonean counterparts were proving to be valuable assets to his administration, and the high quality of University of Sierra Leone degrees, was internationally recognized. We savoured that recognition as we travelled out of the country on exchange visits and conferences.

As soon as I had reported my arrival to the Registrar, I called a meeting of the department's staff. I received a report on progress with arrangements for the new session and briefed them fully on my overseas visits. Not long after my return the Registry called an appointment's committee meeting at which interviews were conducted to fill staff vacancies in a number of departments. In the case of the Department of Engineering, only one candidate, Idrissa Yilla,[25] out of the crop of applications received for lectureship in engineering, was successful in gaining appointment. With money, available for recruitment of additional part-time lecturers, the department obtained approval for the appointment of Mr. Abayomi Griffin[26] as a part-time lecturer in Mechanical Engineering. Mr Griffin had taken his degree from Sheffield and was then the Chief Mechanical Engineer at the Sierra Leone Railways. He joined two others already serving the department. The remaining vacancies would have to be re-advertised. This was a setback, as the teaching load on the few full-time staff would remain well above the college average for a while yet.

Students' Admission and preferential scholarships for Science and Engineering Applicants

The students entering the department in October 1963 were admitted under the same entry conditions as those for the previous diploma. Although many were qualified for entry into the college's science degree programmes, they had chosen engineering even though their final qualification would in the first place be a diploma. In the early years of independence, many students admitted into engineering went through their courses on government scholarships. It was government's policy to offer scholarships to students who could show evidence of a firm offer of admission into the college to study science or engineering. The rapid growth of admission numbers in later years, forced a change in government policy. Gradually more capable students found themselves without sponsorships. As a result, the department set up its own scholarship scheme for such students, raising funds for the scheme from private individuals and non-government organizations.

The re-constituted Faculty of Pure and Applied Sciences became operative that year, and students registering for engineering did so with that faculty following the normal procedures. Students who were successful in their first-year examinations were taken into the revised second year programme which, for the first time, required them to spend three full terms in college to be followed by a three-month intensive industrial training. Students entering their third year received lectures based on the old final year syllabus. This accommodation fitted the situation at the time. Although there was the suggestion from some of our advisers, that students returning from their industrial year should be admitted into the new taught second year to benefit from the advanced training available, that did not receive popular support. However, with that arrangement, the department was set to plunge into an adventurous year ahead.

Overcoming Prejudices against Course Offerings

The teaching load was spread among four full-time and three part-time lecturers. Workshop and laboratory preparation and supervision were undertaken by one chief technician, two junior technicians and two messengers. Pieces of equipment promised by overseas institutions and gifts of text books and reference material from individual well-wishers, duly arrived and increased the teaching and learning facilities available at the department. Now the department had courses designed to produce sub-professional engineers of high quality to satisfy the nation's need for middle level manpower.

"But where are the innovators and the design engineers; the researchers, and the academics whose creative activities these sub-professionals were being trained to support; when do we begin to train those?"

I had put this question to a director of one of the more prosperous mining companies in the country at one of the frequent dinners the Principal hosted for business and professional people. The objective was to interest them in the work of the college and attract funds for specific development areas. The director was in conversation with the Dean of Pure and Applied Sciences, who was describing to him

70

the improvements the department had made to the old diploma course. He also informed him of the plans the department had to produce degree graduates in the near future. I had heard the Dean say,

"There are not enough trained technicians to satisfy the needs of local industries."

"The college should expand its facilities to train more technicians rather than venture into producing degree engineers," the director advised, and replied to my question in a voice that etched his words deeply in my mind.

"We can get better trained engineers and researchers from overseas. High quality research is being conducted in sophisticated institutions all over the world and provide results available for all of us to use."

I didn't think he deserved it, but courtesy made me say,
"I am afraid you miss the point."
He gave me his attention again, and I went on,

"Without innovators, designers, researchers, and academics addressing the special problems of our country, our reliance on other nations for our economic and social development would deepen and our independence would become a shallow achievement."

There were more like him beyond the boundaries of the college who had to be won over to our side.

That side was growing stronger, however. The Ministry of Education had for a long time pursued a policy of awarding scholarships for overseas study in areas of speciality not available in Sierra Leone. As the cost of overseas training increased, the number of scholarships the government could afford dropped significantly, which led to a revision of policy limiting overseas awards only to candidates with A grade passes in at least two subjects taken at their

A level examinations. Many potential engineering degree candidates were therefore obliged to find alternative careers in the basic sciences, or spend years waiting for a chance to win a foreign scholarship. Given this situation, the government and parents began to look to Fourah Bay College to improve its capacity to provide a higher level of training for more capable students. Secondary schools producing A-level science students started to make enquiries about courses in engineering available at the Fourah Bay College. In particular, they wanted to know when engineering degrees could be taken at the college. After a mere eighteen months of our existence, interest was spreading in what the department was doing. It appeared that the banner of academic change was soon to be lifted by a larger and more vocal constituency than the department's small band of visionaries.

Just before the start of the Michaelmas Term, the new faculty board sat for the first time to deal primarily with approvals of September repeat results for non-final years. Faculty boards met at least once a term except for emergencies, when the appropriate notices had to be given. The second time the faculty met, it was at the beginning of the Epiphany Term and it had on its agenda: 'Proposal for the Introduction of Full Degree Courses in Civil, Mechanical and Electrical Engineering.' The proposal was prepared with the advice of Professors Cassie and Evans, who had earlier guided the department through the development of the improved courses for the advanced diploma. The British pattern of the degree would broadly be followed for the Fourah Bay College degree. Apart from a preliminary year course which students entering without A levels would be required to take, there would be three years of study; an intermediate year, a qualifying year, and a final year. The industrial training provided for in the diploma courses would be retained. The degree would meet the standard required for recognition by the three British Engineering Institutions as fulfilling the conditions for exemption from Parts I and II of the institution's professional examinations. General degrees would be offered in the first instance. As the programme developed, further improvements in staffing and laboratory facilities would dictate the pace of advancement to honours courses. Aspects of the programme would reflect local interest and peculiarities. The target date for the start of these courses was the 1965-1966 session.

The meeting was well attended, the atmosphere tense. I presented the proposal, pointing out its merits. The size of the membership of the new faculty worried the engineering representatives, who were grossly outnumbered. The new faculty now included three other science departments,not in the erstwhile Faculty of Applied Science - Zoology, Botany, and Geography. The representatives from Zoology, included a former school friend who had been an outspoken supporter of the department, having been interested in a career in engineering in his schooldays. However, in that crowded room, there was no way any of us could judge the inclination of the rest of the membership. The Dean invited discussion on the proposal. Much the same arguments made against the improved diploma proposal, resurfaced. Under fire, my colleagues and I hammered through key points in our draft that did not seem to be sinking in; cost savings to parents who could not afford overseas education for their children; output of an increased number and better qualified engineers for the productive sectors of the economy; the building of capacities for investigating problems which no other country but ours would have an interest in solving. Up to the mid-point of the discussion, I reckoned we did not yet have the numbers to pass that proposal, for there were unexpected queries relating to the curriculum, issues of timing of the introduction of the programme and other objections, which I thought were motivated by pure prejudice. Suffocated by the barrage of questions, answers, and arguments for and against, being pumped into the air around us, I mentally left that room.

The Harmattan season had descended on the campus. The cold winds of the season had arrived with the load of fine dust particles it had swept off the Saharan sands. We had seen a few dull days since the beginning of January, and the cold weather associated with that time of the year, had been more severe than was usually experienced on this mountain site. The combined effect of those conditions was known to cause irritability in some people. I lessened mine by recalling an incident on campus, not long before the new session started, when the Principal launched a plan to restore the former Governor's lodge at Kortright. This was a house set at the top of the hill overlooking the central campus at Mount Aureol. It had been neglected for decades since being abandoned before World War II and, after the college was re-settled on these hills at the end of the war, had been left isolated from the rest of the residential area around it. Students even referred to it as "the haunted house."

Dr. Davidson Nicol's plan was to make it the official residence of the Principal. Furious at, or perhaps envious of his plan, detractors had sent him discourteous letters opposing it. He had received insults and open attacks at meetings, all intended to damage his image and kill the project. When it became clear to him that the college would not fund the restoration, he had launched an appeal to raise the funds needed from private donors and see the project through. Dr. Davidson Nicol had given his support to our project because he knew that we were fighting for change, that was necessary. He had endured more than we had to deal with, and understood what it was like, trying to change anything, even when it was for the better. I sat there staring through the windows behind the chairman, wondering what we had to do to save that day for him, for us, and indeed for our country.

Experienced chairmen have a way of reading the minds of members who sit in quiet contemplation at meetings. This one was no exception. I heard my name. That stirred me into consciousness, making me realize that some word or comment was required from me. My engineering colleagues quickly briefed me, and I stood up. saying, "Agreed."
"Meeting stands adjourned." The Dean's voice was crisp and loud, but he was obviously exhausted by the verbal heat of the deliberations.

It transpired that in discussing the details of the courses, the Department of Mathematics had objected to the inclusion of certain topics in the intermediate and qualifying year courses, to which their concurrence had not been previously sought. My agreement signified that the proposal should be withdrawn and re-submitted after consultation with the Mathematics Department on the courses in dispute.

The potential involvement of the Mathematics Department seemed to have been under-estimated. The syllabus proposed for degree students in the Intermediate Year differed from the syllabus for diploma students in the second year of their course. What was proposed for qualifying year students, required the Mathematics Department to provide a dedicated course for engineers. The Mathematic Department complained that they did not have the resources to run two streams of mathematics classes for intermediate year diploma and degree students as well as taking on a brand-new course. We set to work on the problems, examining two possible solutions. For the Intermediate Year classes, the two practicable options to avoid a stalemate with the Mathematics Department, would involve merging the two sets of students, one entering directly into the year with A levels, the other entering from the Preliminary year. We could either have the joint class follow the degree mathematics syllabus proposed for the A-level entrants or adopt the diploma syllabus. The contents removed from the Intermediate Engineering syllabus could then be transferred to the Qualifying Year, increasing the load on these students. We sold this idea to the mathematics negotiating team. They were hesitant to accept but agreed to see how it would work out in practice. The decision to increase the mathematics course content of the qualifying year came back to haunt us in later years as some students were unable to cope with the large syllabus which had to be compressed into one year's course of study. The other point of concern for the Mathematics Department was providing separate classes for Qualifying Year engineering students. Short of agreeing to include in the proposal, the recruitment of additional mathematics staff among the new engineering staff positions to be created, it was unlikely that the mathematicians would endorse the proposal. We accepted the inclusion. A compromise had been struck that allowed us to proceed with our plans. One major obstacle had been cleared, but there were more of them clearly positioned before us. The faculty board, the academic board, and the college council, all had to have their say.

The proposal went back to the board at an emergency meeting in April. It still encountered stiff opposition, particularly in respect of the time table for implementation. There were doubts that most of the appointments proposed would have been made in time for the start of the courses in October, 1965. There was a year to go and vacant positions in the 1963-64 budget were about to be filled. It was made clear to the board that at the start of the programme, new admissions would only be into the Preliminary and Intermediate years. Staff recruitment would be phased over the three years of the programme, and so would the investment in equipment and other instructional materials. Our work was done. We had convinced the board that we had a plan that would provide opportunities for many young and talented school leavers to enter an exciting profession with unlimited scope for creativity and enterprise. The board voted to approve the revised proposal and passed a resolution recommending approval of the degree courses to the academic board. We left the meeting satisfied that our struggles over the last two sessions had not been in vain.

Chapter 7

Establishing Full Degree Courses in Engineering

Minor Setbacks; New Opportunities

The session at which the degree programmes were to be introduced, started expectantly, with new admissions into the first and second years of the new diploma courses. However, as the last term of the session drew near, it became apparent that certain events would conspire to deny me the gratification of participating in the final planning stages for the introduction of the degree programme. Most crucial of these, was the receipt of news from the Principal's office that my application for a post-doctoral fellowship was successful. The fellowship was provided by the Hazen Foundation to honour the memory of Kwegyir Aggrey [27] a distinguished African scholar, and was tenable in the United States of America. I was to take up the fellowship the following year. Reflecting on the promise of those years, it must have registered in the minds of our staff, consciously or unconsciously, that while we were striving to get these advanced courses introduced at the college, there could be setbacks to our plans should any one of us leave to advance our academic status in the college. It was known to young lecturers that one's grade was based on one's academic attainments. Rules governing staff categorization were set by the Senate and implemented by the Appointments and Promotions committee. Four grades of staff were then recognized for academic appointments: Lecturer, Senior Lecturer, Reader, and Professor. Lecturer was the lowest rank and Professor the highest. Young Sierra Leonean members of staff, hoping to improve their academic ranking, looked for staff development opportunities to achieve this. It was regular practice for information on such opportunities to be circulated to departments of the college, encouraging staff to take advantage of them. Although I was promoted to the grade of Senior Lecturer that year, I believed that taking up the fellowship would be an advantage to the department in future years.

Accepting this fellowship, which was supported by the Principal, created a situation with which the college had to deal. There were staff vacancies still to be filled in the department. With that knowledge, the Principal directed that one of the remaining vacancies should be filled at the professorial level to enable the department to cope with any unexpected academic problems that might arise during the planning stages for the launching of the degree courses.

The programme for the establishment of full degree courses in Civil, Mechanical and Electrical Engineering, came into effect as planned in the 1965-66 sessions. It was implemented in the department under a single administrative and academic head. Eighteen months of preparation preceded the intake of students into the degree courses. In the last stages of the planning, a new head of department, Professor Derek Whittaker, was recruited from the United Kingdom to succeed me. Before his arrival, I had secured approval for two new members of staff to fill some of the vacancies that were agreed with the college administration as necessary, to run the new diploma courses effectively in the initial years. Students were already in the middle of their upgraded courses. The number of staff in the department had risen from four to six. While the new head of department prepared to lay his stamp on the department, I gave him every support he needed. I worked with him to introduce administrative changes that transferred some responsibility for organizing courses in each of the three disciplines, to a lecturer in that discipline. Unrecognized as such by the college, the department had begun operating sub-departments. The Head of Department's speciality was electrical engineering. His presence had added significantly to the academic strength of the electrical sub-department. I had handed over to him a development blue print which would serve him in good stead as he steered the department towards the establishment of full degree courses a year later.

The new head saw the first set of students successfully taking the upgraded diploma course through to their final year. The first crop of students with the higher diplomas entered the job market in June 1965. They were enthusiastically received with offers of salaries higher than their predecessors. My replacement finalized arrangements for admitting students to the degree programmes, in collaboration with the science departments where students still had to take required courses. When the programme was launched, the first two years of the degree course were run in tandem with the upgraded diploma course. The changes in the administrative structure that allowed some decentralization of the administration were vital in helping the department cope with the increased number of courses that had to be time-tabled and taught within a single department. The college had itself been undergoing structural changes in anticipation of the passing of an act of Parliament creating the University of Sierra Leone from the existing Fourah Bay College and the newly established Njala University College. The university would have a Vice Chancellor, a position that would be held by the Principals of Fourah Bay College and Njala University College in rotation every two years; the first Vice- Chancellor was to be the Principal of Fourah Bay College. I returned to the department from the United States and Britain in January 1967, just before the act was passed. I had spent my leave of absence from the college undertaking academic research in the US and professional advancement in the UK. I was privileged to be on campus during many consultations held with the college authorities and staff, on the formulation of the act to establish the university. Discussions over the structure and equivalence of courses taken at the Fourah Bay College and Njala University College, the two colleges that were to constitute the university, were as acrimonious as those which preceded the establishment of engineering degree courses at Fourah Bay College.

In that same year, the first students admitted into the degree programme in October 1965 were preparing to enter their final year. The college examination regulations required that external examiners should be appointed to review and approve examination questions, answers and marking schemes, before the examinations were taken. After the examinations, they were also required to scrutinize all marked scripts after they had been second marked by internal examiners. The Head of Department had asked my advice on the selection of an external examiner in Civil Engineering. On our first exposure to outsiders, I had felt that the department needed someone who would give us honest assessments as well as provide proper guidance for future improvement. I suggested Professor Evans, my former professor, who had been our department's unofficial adviser during my term of office as Acting Head of Department. An agreed list of proposed external examiners was submitted to Senate and was approved. The programme for their visit was drawn up in consultation with them so that their examining periods could coincide.

It had been a bumpy ride since we set our sights on the objective of training not only diploma but also degree students. Through the initiative and support of the Principal and the dedication of the staff of the department, we were at the point of delivering it. The title of the degree would be, Bachelor of Engineering, with the abbreviation, B.Eng. As agreed, it would be a general degree awarded in three divisions, first, second and third. The staff meetings of the department were a monthly affair, but nearing the period of the examinations they had become weekly. Having part-time lecturers made meeting college deadlines for submission of examination questions, marked examination scripts and final year students' projects difficult, so these meetings were necessary to monitor their progress. At the end of one such meeting, I was invited by the head of department into his office; he wanted to know how I felt about our prospects of going through the examinations without alarming hitches. I volunteered the positive view that we had worked hard enough to be able to sail through without damage.

"Do you think we ought to conduct mock interviews with the final year students before they face the externals?" he asked. I replied,

"I think it will erode their confidence, making them feel that the intent of external examiners is to expose their weaknesses." I pressed the issue.

"Is it not the same thing as finding out how much they know outside their written papers, to justify passing them?"

"No," said Whittaker. "I believe the externals will question the students more about their projects, and their project supervisors will be with them at the interviews."

Having noticed this trend in practice at his old university, Sheffield, Whittaker was less bothered that the interviews could affect the final grading of students. Students' projects counted fully as a subject of the final examination. To pass the examination as a whole, a student had to score a fifty percent mark in that subject. Since the head of department had the advantage of recent experience, I bowed to that.

The examinations that year were as much an assessment of our department, as it was of the students. Since the department was also aiming for international recognition of the degrees, we were required to submit for scrutiny, not only the final year papers, but also the questions and answers of all examinations preceding final year. Students' projects were also submitted for assessment. Once the examination questions were approved by the external examiners as meeting the appropriate standards, they were sent to the college's examinations office for the conduct of the examinations. There were three examiners to satisfy. They should not only report to the Senate on all aspects of the examination, but also on the quality of the physical facilities, equipment, and staff of the department. Clouds of anxiety hung thickly over the department in the weeks before and after the examinations. Ears and eyes waited for the condemnation that all who scorned our daring had predicted. Instead, commendation arrived. There were recommendations for course revision in the second qualifying year, which examiners thought were pitched too high for a general degree, and for some improvement in the existing laboratory facilities. However, the examiners indicated their willingness to sponsor the Bachelor of Engineering degree for recognition by the major British engineering institutions as fulfilling the conditions for exemption from the theoretical parts of the institutions' professional examinations. The Royal Charter granted to Fourah Bay College in January 1960, constituting it as the University College of Sierra Leone, gave the college authority to grant its own degrees. The first graduates in engineering had their University of Sierra Leone degrees conferred in December 1968. It was the Dean of Pure and Applied Sciences, according to tradition, and not the head of department, who had the honour and privilege of presenting the successful students for their awards in the presence of the Principal Nicol, who had facilitated this achievement.

Dr. Davidson Nicol did not see the department advance further. He relinquished the office of Principal at the end of that session, and was succeeded by Professor Harry Sawyerr, a distinguished theologian who was an ordained minister of the Anglican Church, and had risen to the rank of Canon of the Saint George's Cathedral of Freetown. He was a product of Fourah Bay College; B.A. (1934); M.A. (1936), M.Ed. (1940) and had been a member of staff of the college since he was recruited as tutor in 1933. Before his appointment as Principal, he was Vice Principal, and Professor and Head of the Department of Theology. He was well known as a champion of academic excellence at the college, and epitomised it. He took pride in his Durham academic background and had insisted that students of his department be taught Greek, classical theology, and biblical studies, believing that far from being irrelevant to African intellectual development, ignorance of those subjects was detrimental to it. However, in spite of his passion for the humanities, he had been one of the senior academics on campus who supported the introduction of engineering courses. My colleagues and I hoped that his interest in us would increase as he instilled appreciation of excellence in all departments. Principal Harry Sawyerr continued along his predecessor's path and nurtured a department that still had a long way to go towards achieving its full potential.

The following year, the Faculty of Pure and Applied Sciences elected me Dean. My election indicated a reversal of the scepticism with which the department was viewed when it was absorbed into the board. Engineering student numbers had increased. The staff of the department had been buoyed by the engineering students' successes. As a department fighting for recognition, we learnt to spread our message to anyone who cared to listen, in every committee, and at every forum on which we were privileged to sit. We were featured in discussion programmes on radio and television that publicized the role of the engineer in the development of the country. Everyone, it seemed, wanted to know about engineering at Fourah Bay College, and many pupils in science classes in secondary schools in the country, both boys and girls, wanted to study engineering. Because of the passion with which the department presented its cause, it had developed a good rapport with the Principal and his Vice Principal, Dr. Eldred Jones, Professor of English Language and Literature. He, like Canon Harry Sawyer, had earned his first degree from the college, but acquired his higher degrees from Oxford and Durham. He was one of the few professors from the main campus, who would walk down to the engineers' den to see the facilities and enquire about the department's progress. We were surprised at the level of interest he showed in our equipment and experiments till, on one such visit, he revealed that he was no stranger to machines. He had worked in the Sierra Leone Printing Department just after leaving school, when he had no career plans. Having been in an engineering environment before, and having seen engineers at work, he recognized the importance to the country of properly trained engineers. When he later became Principal, Professor Eldred Jones's interest in the engineering department was helpful in obtaining approvals for more improvements. A man of great wit and charm, he was a source of inspiration to junior lecturers, who admired him for his elegance and poise. Apart from establishing himself as an authority on the image of Africa in Elizabethan literature, he was known for his love of music and drama and promoted them in the college, by sponsoring musical performances and producing several memorable plays by African and European writers..

Soon after my election as Dean of the Faculty of Pure and Applied Sciences, the head of department resigned his appointment to take up a new post at the University of Zambia. When the vacancy was advertised by the Inter-University Council (IUC) in the UK, I applied for it along with two other candidates. On the recommendation of the IUC, following the interviews, I was offered the position. As soon as the formalities of my appointment were over, I invited the staff of the department to a brainstorming session to plan the way forward, following the production of our first graduates. Several suggestions were made, some of which we implemented immediately. We sent letters out to foreign-trained Sierra Leonean engineers with post-graduate degrees, whose addresses we could obtain from various contacts, inviting them to join the department as full-time members of staff. The department also proposed the setting up of an advisory committee on engineering education, with a membership that included professional engineers, representatives from industry and the university. Its mandate was to carry out periodic review of our courses and make suggestions for keeping them abreast of new technological advancements. The proposal was endorsed by the faculty board, which stipulated that the committee should report directly to it. To ensure that the department benefitted from the income it received from its testing and consulting activities, it obtained the permission of the new Principal to create a separate account into which its earnings would be paid and from which some of its equipment needs would be met. When the request was sent to the Finance Office for action, it was presented to the newly appointed Finance Officer, Mr. Seray-Wurie; he had succeeded Mr Hamilton, the first African appointed to the post. Seray-Wurie who was known to discourage the creation of multiple accounts within the college, had frowned upon the suggestion from the department when it was first presented to him. However, the green light from the Principal facilitated a turn around. That forward-looking Principal had faith in our team and the direction in which it was moving the department.

In 1970, I was made Vice Principal, succeeding Professor Eldred Jones. This is an elected post at Fourah Bay College. Only full

84

professors could stand as candidates although the entire academic staff of the college was entitled to vote. My candidature was proposed by Professor Edward Blyden III, who had always been a great supporter of mine and a trusted counsellor. It was entirely through his efforts and his influence amongst senior staff at the college, that I was elected to that position. That elevation made it possible for me to sit on decision-making committees. It also gave me direct access to the Principal, a privilege that enabled engineering needs to be given the priority they deserved. Even in such positions of privilege, a wrong move or approach could be detrimental to one's interests. Therefore, whenever necessary, I was cautious to use a softer line of approach in making the department's case than I had done before my election. Working closely with Principal Harry Sawyerr, was exhilarating. He was dynamic, mentally sharp, and uncompromisingly outspoken. The Vice Principal's responsibilities included superintending student affairs, working with the student wardens. As Vice Principal under Dr. Davidson Nicol, Professor Sawyerr had earned respect from his peers not only for his academic achievements but for his stand on discipline on the campus. I frequently sought his advice in tackling student problems and benefitted enormously from his guidance. Nevertheless, there were occasions when students fanned flames of discontent that challenged our joint efforts to contain. Yet, in times of crises as in periods of tranquillity, the Principal put students first. He kept an open house from which he dispensed love and charity to every student who came to his door, as considerate to them as he was to the college's senior and junior staff.

Further Expansion and Staff Development

Under Principal Sawyerr, the Engineering Department experienced significant improvements to its physical infrastructure and laboratory facilities. Through his efforts, the department became one of the beneficiary departments at Fourah Bay College of the British Council Academic Link Scheme. Our participation in this scheme enabled us to receive visiting lecturers and professors from universities with which we had established links. It also gave opportunities to junior academic staff to undergo post-graduate studies in link departments. Harry Sawyerr proved to be a man who was quick to act. In many instances the department received prompt response to appeals for his intervention on pressing matters affecting its progress. In February 1971, as a result of one of those appeals, he made the administration implement the department's long standing request for a new engineering building to relieve the cramped conditions under which it ran courses. The number of students then stood at 153 and was rising with the popularity of the courses. That request had previously been approved by the Planning and Development Committee, subject to the availability of funds, but had not then been acted upon. The committee had hoped that appeals would be made to overseas donors for assistance in implementing the project. As it was becoming difficult to attract funds from overseas donors for such a development, the Principal authorized the construction of the new building from college funds. That same year, he supported an increase in the department's equipment budget and staff complement, permitting it to increase course options. As a result, the electrical engineering degree course was expanded, enabling students to offer one of two options of specialization, namely, power engineering and electronics. In addition, new courses in Public Health Engineering and Transportation Engineering were introduced as options in Civil Engineering, and Industrial Management became an option for students taking Mechanical Engineering.

On instructions from the Principal, the College Architect, Mr. George Lewis, the first Sierra Leonean to hold the post, received the commission to put up the building which would be his first project. He began preparing the preliminary plans in June 1971, with a brief developed in consultation with the department and the Estates and Building Committee. The building would have three floors: a mezzanine floor, a ground floor and a lower ground floor. Vehicular access would be provided to both ground floors to facilitate deliveries of heavy machinery and equipment. Before work started on the preliminary design, the department had proposed to the Estates and Building Committee that the components of the design relating to the structural, mechanical and electrical engineering aspects of the building be designed by the department's fully registered professional engineers. The cost to the college, we indicated, would be minimal and would relate to drafting charges for the additional draughtsmen that would be required to produce detailed drawings in the College Architect's office. The committee rejected our proposal after an intense argument about the department's professional competence. At one stage of the discussion, the Architect, in an emphatic statement delivered with a voice that sounded like a contralto missing his notes, "I don't want student exercises called designs."

Previous commissions had been carried out by the British Architects, Frank Rutter and Partners. George Lewis had been given the opportunity to practice his profession without doubts being cast upon his capabilities; yet there he was, denying that opportunity to others. I had words in my mind to return the slight, but spared him the greater insult that had been couched in the words my lips were ready to deliver.

In a twist to this saga, when the final draft of the construction plan was presented to the Estates and Building Committee, those of us representing the department detected a flaw in the roof design. It had drains running inside the building, just abutting the inner face of its long sides, to present a façade that concealed the roof. Concealed roofs had become popular around that time, but several incidents had been reported of serious leaks in buildings with this type of roof. In some cases, the department had been called to advise contractors on remedial measures. Our hydraulics specialist therefore advised against the concept presented, pointing out that the depth and slope of the drains would be inadequate to carry the runoff from the roof at peak periods of the rainy season. Our advice was ignored. There would be many more occasions when the department and its staff would have to face such walls of prejudice. Fortunately, attitudes changed over the years and the faculty is now fully involved in the design and supervision of aspects of the physical renovation of the college.

In later years, I discovered the source of Professor Harry Sawyerr's respect for the sciences. L. M. Miles's [28] abridged biography of Harry Sawyerr, referred to the influence on him of Bishop T. S. Johnson. Sawyerr had embraced the bishop's vision for a comprehensive education, which included science, theology, economics and Greek. Miles explained that Sawyerr, like Johnson, considered science or economics alone, insufficient to take Sierra Leone to its rightful place in the world. While these disciplines were important, both Johnson and Sawyerr believed that ignorance of European intellectual streams, would be more detrimental to African intellectual development, than would be the idea that such forms of study were irrelevant to Africa. That was the vision that helped Sawyerr to accommodate ideas across the divisions of academic disciplines as existed at Fourah Bay in his day, and allowed engineering a respected place among them.

In 1972, an act of Parliament was passed giving effect to the recommendations of the review of the 1967 act, setting up the University of Sierra Leone. Under the provisions of the act, the positions of Principal of Fourah Bay College, the Principal of Njala University College, and the Vice Chancellor of the University of Sierra Leone were separated. Apparently, the review had concluded that the provisions of the act passed in 1967, had proved unworkable, for it had been noticed that the rotational Vice Chancellorship bred animosity between the two principals. Each principal believed the other to be biased in favour of his own college in the disbursement of grants and other benefits, when it was his turn to hold the post, and that the provision of opportunities for staff advancement was subject to the same bias. The new act created a unitary system in which all college departments and institutes were answerable to a full-time Vice Chancellor. As a result, academic matters once dealt with by the principals, became the responsibility of the Vice Chancellor, as well as the centralized administration of the entire university. Principals were only responsible for what were called domestic matters. Professor Arthur T. Porter, a former professor at the college, was appointed to the post. Professor Harry Sawyerr remained Principal of Fourah Bay College and Dr Sahr Matturi remained Principal of

Njala University College. Dr. Porter had been away from Fourah Bay College since 1962, when he was invited to serve as Principal of the University College of East Africa and later as Vice Chancellor of the University of Nairobi. He was returning to Fourah Bay College from a university with a large faculty of engineering, and so knew the scale of the resources required to service a fully operational engineering faculty.

The Department of Engineering welcomed that appointment. Working with the new Vice Chancellor, Professor Sawyerr encouraged the further development of the college even though in the restructured university, he had become answerable to him. He ensured that work on the construction of the new engineering building started in earnest in January 1972. On nearing the completion of the building the decision of a suitable paint for the students' workshop became an issue that needed to be referred to the Estates and Building Committee, because of a variation from the works contract and its cost implication. The department had suggested that with the grease and muck that would be thrown around by inexperienced students, it would be advisable to have the walls of that workshop overlaid with a high quality washable paint to facilitate washing down and restoring badly soiled portions of the walls. The recommendation went to the College Council from the Estates and Building Committee; on that occasion, with the support of the Architect. Again, questions were raised about the justification for such an expense, even though it had been explained that in the long term, there would be savings. It appeared that the acquisition of a new building by the department had upset our diehard opponents, and they had mobilized outside support to throw the proposal out of the window. A representative of the Alumni Association displayed more aggression than most, often speaking after the staff critics leading the attack. As she was sitting down after a barrage of condemnation, she ranted,
"We don't want painted palaces called workshops."
Wisdom prevailed, however. Chairing that meeting was the Chancellor of the University, Sir Samuel Bankolé Jones, a distinguished jurist and former Chief Justice of Sierra Leone. He

appreciated the practicality of the proposal and advised that it be supported. The wall treatment proposed was finally approved.

The new building was formally opened on 15th March, 1974, by the Hon. N. A. P. Buck, Minister of Works, deputizing the Vice President and Prime Minister, Hon. S. I. Koroma. Principal Sawyerr' whose bold decision had led to the construction of the building, had by then retired. He was succeeded in office by Professor Eldred Jones who presided over the opening. The building was an impressive three-storey structure with a mezzanine floor. The mezzanine floor provided accommodation for the Head of Department and eight other members of staff, two lecture rooms, a library/documents room, a staff room and a kitchen. Part of the ground floor was designed to accommodate the heavy structures laboratory, with space provided for installing a 1000kN Avery Universal Testing Machine. The rest of the floor would accommodate, three other laboratories, a students' workshop and a main workshop to serve the needs of all sections of the department. The lower ground had more staff offices and space to accommodate mechanical engineering laboratories. The task of furnishing and equipping the building was left to the department. The summer of 1973 was spent trying to cope with that task. We identified overseas suppliers which would satisfy our equipment machinery requirements and made requisitions for furniture from the college's furniture workshop, headed by Mr Alfred Sonah. There was no furniture, however intricate the shape, that his skilled hands and those of his staff could not make. Before orders were confirmed, the college arranged for me to visit prospective manufacturers of equipment and machinery we had requested. Apart from some production machines and a heavy duty universal testing machine, included in our shopping list, we were keen to equip our student's workshop with the most modern machines. Accompanied by our Chief Technician and a representative of the Crown Agents, the college's procurement agents, I visited the factories of the major equipment and workshop machine manufacturers in the UK over a period of two weeks. Once the orders were confirmed, we returned to the department to organize the transfer of laboratories and offices that had been improperly housed. By October, 1974, we had occupied much of the space provided. We then had to wait for the arrival and commissioning of the new equipment. It took another year for the building to be fully equipped and all sections of the department functioning effectively.

When Professor Porter assumed office in 1973, he embarked on a review of the country's education at a series of conferences held between 1973 and 1976. The university implemented some of the recommendations of that review with international help. During the first five years of his vice chancellorship, Professor Porter, established new institutes within the colleges and made the influence of Fourah Bay College felt within the various constituent arms of the university. He also endeavoured to make the distinction between the university and its colleges physically noticeable on the Fourah Bay College campus by erecting a central administration building on which he named 'University House'. The erection of University House so close to the college's own administrative building blurred somewhat the distinction the Vice Chancellor had intended to make. The Principal of the college may have found this nearness unsettling, but his departments found it convenient to have the academic head of the university close by. When Professor Eldred Jones became principal, the department was gratified that another of its supporters had assumed office as head of the college. The department had more ladders to climb to reach the summit of its aspirations and hoped Principal Jones would work in concert with the Vice Chancellor.

Since launching the improved diploma course and improving its laboratory facilities, the department had been making an impact on the community with its industrial testing and consulting work. With the college's approval, it had developed its testing unit into a recognized consulting centre, named 'Advisory Services in Technology Research and Development' (ASTRAD). By 1973, ASTRAD had been involved in, and coordinated 18 (eighteen) research projects undertaken by staff members, which were directly related to national development. It had become an important building materials research and development unit in the country. It had successfully designed and constructed many promising low cost products, including, agricultural equipment for use at village level, screw presses for extraction of palm oil from the fruit, and solar water heaters, which were undergoing preliminary tests. Slowly the college was recognizing the creative and engineering potential of the department. After years of denial of this capacity, the college offered the department its first commission in 1975. It was to design a small incinerator for the disposal of refuse collected within the campus. More commissions followed this initial breakthrough, after it had been made clear to the college, that the design teams at ASTRAD were constituted from the most experienced professionally licensed engineers from the department. However, from time to time questions about the unit's responsibility for its designs were raised by the Estates and Building Committee, perhaps intended to interrupt the flow of engagements from the college to the department.

Chapter 8

Creating a National Structure for Engineering Education

Rationalizing the Engineering Education System

The struggle to introduce relevant courses at a university becomes harder in an environment with scarce resources and multiple priorities. With so much being classed as priority, personal struggles are inevitable during competition among functionaries to secure a share of these resources. The interesting thing about managing resources is that in trying to do what is right, compromises often come in the way and force dilution of treasured objectives to get the concurrence of the opposition. This usually hurts the cause of progress. In the early stages of independence of former European colonies in Africa, interest in the application of science and technology to achieve enhanced standards of living and productivity was subordinated to promoting political and cultural re-awakening. While this indifference to the importance of science and technology continued into later years, the character of these twin agents of progress and prosperity, had become more complex and baffling. Accomplishments in science and technology were being recorded daily in every aspect of human life, unlocking many of the secrets of nature, and holding out promises of comfort, wealth, and happiness to the entire world. Africa's contribution to the generation of that stock of new knowledge and skills, was paltry and the situation since independence had not changed. This poor level of contribution had affected Africa's image and socio-economic standing, in a world dominated by knowledge-intensive development and industrial competitiveness. It is therefore vital that training to develop local capacities be tailored to meet the challenges of joining the mainstream of modern scientific and technological advancement, and contributing to the stock of new knowledge, particularly that

93

which multiplies output from productive activity. Yet, we had entered the decade of the nineteen seventies offering degree courses which did little to stimulate creativity in students taking them. This was raising concern nationally. On the other hand, products of the diploma programme were gaining more acceptability in industry than were their degree counterparts.

Other African countries were experiencing similar crises of confidence in the various national systems that were producing science and engineering graduates. Concern for the state of affairs and the inaction of African countries to improve the situation, was brought into sharper focus when a series of country surveys were conducted in the early 1970s by the United Nations Economic Commission for Africa (UNECA). These surveys provided the data on which the commission's strategy for a World Plan of Action, [29] to address the needs and priorities in African Region was based. The surveys revealed that after ten or so years of consciousness of the new responsibilities of nationhood, there was still a general weakness in the Science and Technology infrastructure in the region, and particularly in the machinery for decision making in Science and Technology matters. This inability to create the necessary science and technology infrastructure for rapid development, was stifling progress in the development sectors of national economies. The World Plan of Action was intended to spearhead new efforts during the United Nations Second Development Decade, to institute measures for bringing about needed development through the meaningful application of science and technology. Some of these measures involved attempts, aimed at the creation of necessary Government organs for deliberating on scientific and technical affairs. They also involved, policy-making, initiating, orientating and expanding research activities. It was hoped that these would help nations acquire the necessary technologies for increasing productivity. The success of the World Plan of Action was difficult to assess by any direct method.

However, the findings, of the United Nations ECA mission sent out in 1978 to a number of African countries, for identifying a suitable host country for the African Regional Centre for Technology indicate to some degree, the level of achievement in certain sectors during the period of operation of the Plan. The mission identified several national structures which had been set up for Science and Technology policy-making and planning, including national research councils, and institutions for advanced training and research. But the mission discovered that there was still little accomplished over the period in creating an informed public in science and technology; little done towards the introduction of science development planning, as a support activity to social development planning, particularly in the development of national plans for the transfer of commercial technology, and that much less still had been achieved in establishing some formal machinery for effecting national science and technology development. Despite the enormous display of support and encouragement from major world bodies, manifested in proposals and projects, such as those in the World Plan of Action itself, and in such resolutions, such as those of the OAU Council of Ministers (September 1967 and September 1968) and the UNESCO and OAU conferences on Education and Scientific and Technical Training, in relation to Development in Africa (1968), the decade of the seventies witnessed no technical progress, which one could see reflected in any improved state of the region's economy.

According to the World Bank, the decade was one of slow overall economic growth for most countries. Coupled with other alarming indications of economic danger, the World Bank records show that during the period, 15 countries recorded negative rates of growth of income per capita, and output per capital rose more slowly in the seventies than in the sixties, when even the rate was the slowest in the world. While there were external constraints affecting Africa's economic progress, these could have been overcome by greater vigilance in planning. Developing African countries have always quoted the damaging impact of the world economic recession, escalating oil prices, severe terms-of-trade loss for mineral exports, and trade restrictions imposed by developed countries, as the main external factors affecting their economies. However, the facts are that many of these external constraints operated in most other developing regions outside Africa, but they were able to overcome them and expand their economies. Indeed, by the end of the decade, the African nations themselves, had carried out a self-evaluation of their development and had concluded that something more effective than had hitherto been done, was necessary to bring about meaningful economic and social development of their countries.

Heads of State and Government of the region had been struggling with ways to mobilize science and technology for the development of their countries, but projections of progress had been disappointing. Growth in per capita income for countries in the region had been low. If the seventies were bad, the projections for the years following were even more pessimistic. These projections have made it imperative for all countries in the region to ensure that the World Plan of Action works. It is the responsibility of the wider community of nations, to prevent the collapse of what was regarded, at the eve of political independence of the African nations, as the 'Africa Experiment'. The acceptance of the right of nations to govern themselves, must necessarily imply the acceptance of the right of those same nations to create for their peoples, the necessary conditions for eking a decent standard of living. The international community, therefore, has a role to play in providing whatever moral and material support it can muster to join in the renewed efforts to be pursued for the attainment of the goals set in the World Plan of Action and other African inspired plans.

Unease about the future of the African peoples has been felt by a number of private and Government agencies in the developed world. Expressions of support for change in the region have taken several forms, including grants, direct loans, export credits, supply of experts, equipment, materials, and information. Such support measures have emanated from solutions of problems of African underdevelopment identified and investigated in advanced countries eager to render assistance. These endeavours are no doubt laudable. However, they conflict with the aspirations in pronouncements of African policy leaders that Africa should cultivate the virtue of self-reliance among member states.

In fact, it was well understood by developing countries, if not by the developed ones, that research conducted in developed countries to determine solutions to problems in developing countries, take insufficient account of the immense complexity of the problems for which solutions are required. In many cases their findings ignore the social and environmental dimensions of the problems. International cooperation which permits and promotes the utilization of local talent and resources, encourages development of local capacities, and supports local and regional efforts to achieve scientific and technological progress, is the cooperation for self-reliance which Africa often speaks of today. This is the cooperation that recognizes the passionate desire of the peoples of the region for change. It will also restore dignity to a people kept so long in humble dependence on the rest of the world for the means of exercising its rights to develop itself. And this includes the capacity to carry out research activities. These are recognized as vital in the development process and cannot be relegated to investigators who do not possess the sensitivity for tackling the region's problems.

Only carefully planned and executed research programmes can result in innovation, or lead to successful production. In this respect, understanding of these sentiments is not always easy. Few developed countries are committed enough to the goals of African development, to give assistance on those terms. Canada is one of the few. In 1970, the Canadian parliament created the International Development Research Centre (IDRC), with the expressed objective to support research designed to adapt science and technology to the needs of developing countries. Within this institutional framework, the country financed research in agriculture, food and nutrition sciences, social sciences and communications. It recognized the need for international cooperation which promotes self-reliance, by addressing itself to the solution of problems in major areas of need in developing countries, including problem-solving capability within countries in Asia, Latin America, the Middle East and Africa; thus, helping them to solve their problems.

In Sierra Leone, the gap in the technical manpower structure at the middle grade level, continued to be recognized by maintaining the diploma programme in the three main engineering branches, Civil, Electrical and Mechanical, and providing more practical workshop training within the course. The programme was run side by side with the general degree course. Unfortunately, as degree holders were proving their worth in industry and earning good salaries, a large number of diploma holders began to seek access to degree qualifications in the country or overseas which then moved them up from the technician to the professional engineer's grade. There was, therefore, a concern that if this situation continued, the shortage of trained higher technicians would become acute; engineers would then find themselves having to perform tasks usually assigned to technicians as well as undertaking design and research activities. In anticipation of this outcome, the department undertook the development of a unified structure for the education and training of Technicians and Engineering. This unique plan was intended to integrate all training in the country related to engineering. All students would start their education at the Freetown Technical Institute or a similar technical college to gain technician training and expertise before taking a degree course at the university.

One of the most significant conclusions from the findings of the conference on the review of education in Sierra Leone, was that there was an urgent need for a significant increase in opportunities for technical and vocational education [30]. The conferences assessed the best long-term pattern for educational development of the country, and redefined the university's role as an instrument of national development. The department presented its unified course strategy at these conferences and contributed to the discussions which led to the conclusions recorded in the final report, entitled 'All Our Futures'. The conference endorsed the plan. We believed that armed with those conclusions the Vice Chancellor would add his significant influence to Principal Jones's, in order to give the department the tools it needed to further strengthen its capacity to play its role in a university redefined as an instrument for national development.

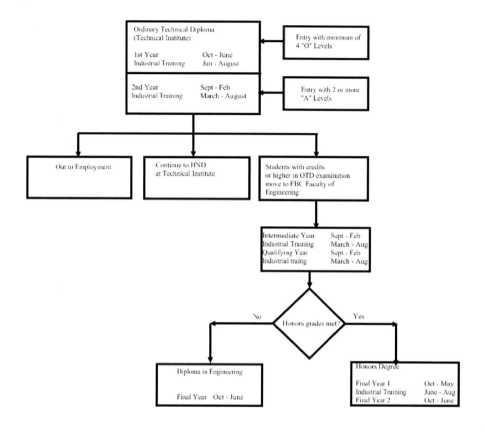

Figure 1: Proposed Unified Structure for the Training of Technicians and Engineers for Sierra Leone.

The plan shown in Figure 1, outlines a programme divided into two parts. The first part was to be undertaken at the Freetown Technical Institute and the second part in the proposed Faculty of Engineering at Fourah Bay College. All students would enter the Freetown Technical Institute to pursue a two-year Ordinary Technician Diploma (OTD) course. The minimum entry requirements would be four relevant 'O' levels, as operated for Diploma students at Fourah Bay College. Students with two A level

99

passes at the General Certificate of Education (GCE) would be given exemptions from part of the OTD course to enable them to complete it in one year. Students leaving school at Form Five without the relevant 'O' level passes would take a special examination for aptitude and academic competence and, if successful, would be admitted into the Technical Institute's OTD programme.

At the end of the Ordinary Technicians Diploma, students who passed with credit or distinction, would proceed to Fourah Bay College to read for the three-year diploma in Engineering or the four-year honours degree, depending on their grades. Students not qualified to enter FBC, would either spend an extra year at the Technical Institute for an award of the Higher Technicians Diploma, or enter the job market. This arrangement would ensure that most university entrants had a good practical engineering background allowing them to function as technicians if necessary. The arrangement would also ensure that dropouts from the university courses would be employable, having already had a practical qualification.

This new approach to training would overcome the difficulty experienced by the department in providing industrial attachment with local companies, for students entering the engineering course straight from school. Such students had to undergo industrial training only at designated levels during their academic work, but their lack of initial hands-on experience with machine tools made most local firms unwilling to accept them for short-term training, and when they did so, were sometimes unwilling to pay them any allowance during their attachment. Several attempts were made through seminars and visits to industries, to reach an understanding of the problems involved and find solutions to them, but the department never succeeded in finding the ideal solution.

During the development of the structure, the department received advice from the Sierra Leone Institution of Engineers (SLIE), and support for its implementation. This was the time when concern was growing about the technical skills gap in the region, and the ineffectiveness of measures implemented by African engineering institutions, like ours, to narrow it. Aware of this situation, particularly in respect of relevance in the training being offered, the Department of Engineering, in cooperation with the SLIE, proposed within the unified structure, an extension of the duration of all programmes by one year. The honours degree course would fit into the programme, and more subject specialization would be introduced in areas such as production engineering, chemical engineering, radio and television engineering, industrial electronics, communication systems, power systems, engineering structures, soil mechanics and foundation engineering, traffic and transportation engineering, hydrology, and public health engineering. All courses would to be made relevant to the needs of Sierra Leone, and highlight local problems.

Compromise Programme: Responding to failure to implement Unified Structure.

Unfortunately, the Ministry of Education was concerned about the managerial and resource requirements that would be necessary at the Technical Institute, to implement the structure. Endorsement of the unified programme by the ministry at that time was proving problematic, and was slowing down the process of restructuring, which the department believed was vital for the establishment of a strong training base for all levels of technicians and engineers. These changes were expected to take place at an opportune moment when the honours programmes were being introduced.

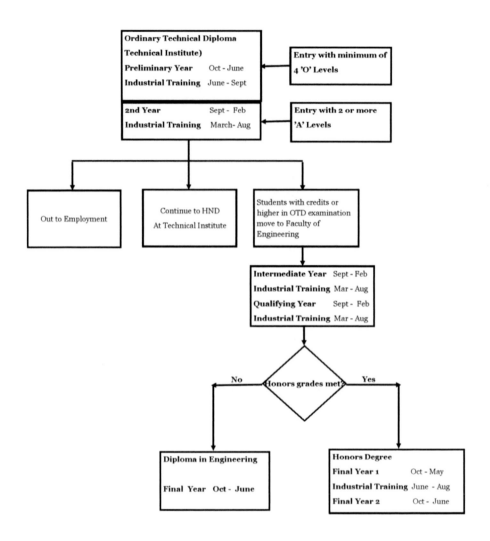

Figure 2: Compromise Structure for Honours Degree and Diploma in Engineering

It became clear that the department would have to find an alternative way to incorporate some of the ideas in the national scheme into its course structure for the honours degree, so as to achieve the best possible training for the nation's technicians and engineers of the future. The modification outlined in Fig. 2 was the solution adopted. The department was eager to move on to the establishment of its honours courses and would not be held back by trying to sell a national programme

After years of intense debate about the importance of appropriate industrial training for students, and how to provide it effectively, it appears that at last a consensus is emerging amongst professional engineers in the country. The current view among professional engineers is to present to the national government, a proposal drawn up by the Sierra Leone Institution of Engineers, for the introduction of an Industrial Training Levy, [31] through an act of Parliament. Under the act, firms would be required to pay it, based on an assessment acceptable to the Sierra Leone Chamber of Commerce and Industry. A training fund would be created out of the levy, and firms joining the scheme would be encouraged to accept students for training by receiving a subsidy for that purpose.

Chapter 9

Founding of the Faculty of Engineering

Upgrading Degree Courses

The department aimed to establish engineering courses that ranked as highly among similar courses in African universities as courses in other departments. We continued our work on the restructuring of the courses, eliminating that part of our original plan, which included training at the Technical Institute. We concentrated our attention on the further upgrade of our existing degree courses to honours level. This was becoming urgent, as students from the region were beginning to apply for admission into degree courses in the department. Introduction of honours courses would further increase the department's popularity and solidify the gains of past years. In pursuance of this, we solicited advice from our external examiners and engineering faculties of British universities with which we had established links. Prior to this, we had carried out an evaluation of the existing courses and assessed the existing teaching and laboratory facilities. The outcome enabled us to determine the level of restructuring required and the additional resources that would be adequate to start a credible honours programme in the department.

Joining the department in this review and assessment exercise were the department's three external examiners, J. E. Houldin, Professor of Electrical Engineering from Chelsea College, University of London, A. R. Cusens, Professor of Civil Engineering from the University of Dundee, and Dr. D. J. Ryley of the University of Liverpool. The evaluation report brought to light a number of weaknesses. In particular, students in the intermediate and qualifying years of both the diploma and degree courses were overloaded with learning materials. Some of them were found either to be of little local relevance, or inappropriate to be taught to students at that

104

stage of their training. Course improvements were suggested for which approval was obtained from the Pure and Applied Sciences Faculty and Senate. In the 1974-75 session, we implemented the recommendations. We revised course contents in some of the subjects taken in the intermediate and qualifying years and introduced topics of direct local relevance. We extended the duration of design and drawing classes to improve students' creative and drawing skills. The advice of the reviewers was that with the modification made, we would have in place, the first two years of the honours degree programme, following the Preliminary year. The review report also provided a list of requirements and guidelines for structuring the remaining honours courses. All these guidelines and requirements were incorporated in a proposal submitted to the Faculty of Pure and Applied Sciences, after it had received the blessing of the Committee on Engineering Education.

The proposal was discussed at a meeting of the board in April 1976. Among its objectives, was the establishment of a Faculty of Engineering, initially with three departments. When the proposal was presented to the board, it was greeted with derision. From the rear of the room came a muted cry, "Engineering again!"
I had by then relinquished the deanship of the faculty. and was seated in a row with, John McCormack, the department's lecturer in Electrical Engineering, an ardent lieutenant on our fighting team. Others on that row were, B. B. Ibrahim and N. J. Garber, Senior Lecturers, who later became professors in the department. For months, these three had worked selflessly to prepare the proposal document which had been commended by our advisers. At the sound of that awkward cry, our eyes turned to scan the room and I was about to call for order and decorum to be observed when I remembered that I was no longer dean. We tried to assess the threat to our persons, as well as to our proposal. A group of regular critics had already assembled.
"God," I said to my colleagues, "they look smug in their intention to dismiss this." My colleagues shrugged.

105

That cry summed up the frustration felt by our critics at the regularity of our submissions to the board. For our supporters, these submissions carried the ingredients for the transformation of the college from a beacon of enlightenment only, to a blend of that and those creative instruments which would provide perpetual stimulus for national development. The department was ready to face the ultimate test of its will to fight a vital cause. This was 1976. Every barrier to our progress that had been erected before, seemed so impenetrable then; similarly so, did this new and possibly final hurdle. But the department was stronger than ever. Our proposal outlined our achievements. Our staff complement was higher and more impressive than it was, when we first recommended improvements to the old diploma course. There were enough senior academics to provide ,leadership for the proposed honours degree programme. Already, three professors in three disciplines, two of them visiting professors, and four senior lecturers were directing our steady academic advancement. With sixteen new appointments made in the last two sessions, we showed that we had enough staff to man the three separate departments that would comprise the new faculty, while meeting the minimum staff requirement for academic departments. In addition, the department's progress had been noticed internationally and recognized, as evidenced by its hosting of international scholars, mostly from the Inter-University Council of the United Kingdom.

In recent years, our representation at faculty board meetings had grown substantially with the increase in our staff. More science faculty members than before, had joined our campaign for improvements to the old engineering curriculum. Their cooperation extended to their department's involvement in the activities of the engineering open days, which we launched in 1963. These were attracting increasing numbers of senior pupils and teachers from secondary schools in the country. In the previous session, over four hundred pupils were taken on conducted tours of the department's laboratories. They witnessed demonstrations on selected pieces of engineering equipment, and were shown ongoing staff and students' research projects.

The department had presented a well reasoned case and defended it. Why the degree was needed? How we had parcelled the course offerings? Where the target entry material was? What the employment prospects for the products were? What the cost was to the university? And, how would we sell the products to industry? All this had been given in black and white and repeated in verbal statements during the presentation of our document. If incisive minds still had issues to raise, we were ready to debate them and were confident of success. After trying to shoot the proposal down with over an hour of "engineering bashing", our opponents seemed to lose their nerve, for they. failed to table a motion to reject the proposal. The proposal passed the board and was sent to the Senate for approval. Senate deliberated on it just days before the end of the third term. We had timed the process well. If confirmed, the department would be able to give the statuary year's notice as required by the University for the Introduction of new programmes.

The painful realization that opposition could still be mounted against the proposal, dawned on me as the date for the Senate meeting approached. Often, imaginings are worse than reality. So, incidents imagined are open to exaggeration. I expected the worse, hoping the opposite would occur. The limitation of membership of Senate to heads of department and a small representation from faculty boards, encouraged a balanced view of issues to be expressed. Moreover, it was deemed irregular for faculty members to take positions at Senate contrary to recommendations from the board they represented. Nevertheless, it was not unusual for such desertions to take place, as sanctions for such behaviour, if ever applied by deans, were never made public.

I attended the Senate meeting with one of the faculty representatives chosen from our department, prepared to face whatever fate awaited our proposal. The matter of the creation of a Faculty of Engineering was the first item on the agenda. After dealing with the last meeting's minutes and matters arising from them, the Vice Chancellor seating as chairman of Senate, invited presentation and

107

discussion of the engineering proposal. I presented the main points in the proposal. It attracted only a few comments, many of them constructive. After all the worrying thoughts that had invaded my mind, the reality seemed to be different, until the chairman threw some searching questions at us. Technically, they were supposed to be answered by the Dean and the Head of Department, but I, and the other engineers at the meeting, felt responsible for plugging any hole in our bucket. One of our department's representatives was on his feet before I could take in the surprise.

"We have presented a total package for approval, because no one part of the proposal would work effectively without the other; all of the features in the proposal are interdependent."

The chairman had questioned the wisdom of including the honours programme, the establishment of independent departments and the creation of a new faculty in a single proposal for approval. My colleague's answer tallied with the one I would have given.

I had been at previous Senate meetings, where the Vice Chancellor kept everyone in a light-hearted mood, by injecting subtle humour into the proceedings. On this occasion, however, tension undermined my confidence as more members became interested in the discussion on the size of the package of changes to be approved. Meetings do not always go the way one wants them, and this was true of that one.
"Is the department not proposing too sweeping a change?" Someone behind me asked, not really expecting a reply.
When a reply came, it was from the chair, and implied that questions at meetings should relate to specific matters in the proposal that needed clarification. It took me several moments to realize that he was on our side. It was clear that the real sticking point in the proposal, was the creation of the new faculty and not the introduction of the new honours courses or the establishment of three separate departments. That was confirmed when the chairman asked why the department did not want to stay in the present faculty. That was the question no one wanted to ask but everyone

wanted answered. As if being primed, members of staff of the engineering department representing the faculty, took the floor to make their feelings known, explaining that past experiences did not justify the department's continued membership of the Faculty of Pure and Applied Sciences.

Those impassioned contributions to the discussion, seemed to have convinced the chairman and the majority of the members that it would indeed be advantageous for the department to step out of the constrictions of its present home, and expand in an environment in which there would be harmony, and twinning of ideas between colleagues of like minds and interests. The proposal was approved by a significant majority. Later, that decision received the endorsement of the University Court. The Faculty of Engineering had become a reality. We reminded ourselves that the real work would now begin, for we had to produce honours graduates of a high.quality. As far as implementing the honours degree course was concerned, we had one advantage; we were already half way there. It would be a five-year course with specialization in any of the three disciplines, during the last two years, and would replace the general degree. The first three years were already in place; the ,Preliminary, Intermediate and Qualifying. The present third, or final, year would be replaced by a new two-year final, Final Honours I and II, the structure adopted by the older departments.

In later years, the faculty has found it necessary to re-introduce the general degree. On the wisdom of that decision, it is still early to make a judgement. Setting up the departments and appointing heads to manage their affairs, electing a dean and providing him with office, was more challenging. However, the department had already established sub-departments in an internal structure that provided some separation of the disciplines, with a senior staff member of at least the rank of senior lecturer, being assigned limited academic responsibility for each of them. Relationships between staff of all disciplines were good. Everyone understood that we had to work in unity, to achieve a smooth transition to a faculty.

Preparation for the Final Stages of the Transition

We held several planning meetings at which we decided on objectives and actions, and distributed responsibilities. With a year to go, there was time to advertise and fill the posts of Professor and Head of the departments of each of the three departments, Civil, Mechanical and Electrical Engineering.

It was assumed that since my discipline was Civil Engineering, and I was at the time the current Head of Department, it would not be necessary to advertise the headship of the Civil Engineering Department. This had indeed been the expectation of the Vice Chancellor and the Secretary and Registrar of the University. Technically the two posts of Head of Department of Civil Engineering and Professor of Civil Engineering could be filled either by a single candidate, or by two separate candidates. At Fourah Bay, a recent new policy had been introduced, which considered the title of professor, an academic rank, and the head of department an administrative post, which could be filled by a candidate of the rank of Senior Lecturer and above. A candidate of lower rank filling that post, would carry the title of 'Acting Head'. Rumours had been rife since the start of our journey to that stage of our achievement, that my real motive for launching the campaign to establish a Faculty of Engineering at Fourah Bay College, was selfish; that creating educational opportunities for young people from secondary schools was of less importance to me, than achieving my ambition to be foundation dean of a new faculty. We had worked hand in hand with a dedicated staff to achieve this, ignoring the several attempts made by opposing forces to degrade the mission that had consumed so much of our patience and mental energy. I have always held the belief that those who lead missions of change should step aside at the end of their missions and allow others with fresh ideas, to implement them. That belief inspired my decision to decline the opportunity to fill the positions of Head of Department of Civil Engineering and Dean of the Faculty of Engineering. Babatunde B. Ibrahim was appointed the first Head of Department of Civil Engineering and Nicholas J. Garber, the foundation dean of the new Faculty of Engineering. They carried the torch of promise throughout their years of service in those offices, and passed it on to their successors with faith in their will to maintain what they had inherited.

I look back now on that momentous day when Senate approved the creation of the Faculty of Engineering, and wonder how we ever succeeded in lighting that torch of promise on grounds that so badly needed it yet, shunned its presence. I feel satisfied that the determination to effect change and advance the course of engineering in Sierra Leone, has continued unabated from one generation of engineering academics to the next. They have turned out products in increasing number and quality, and given justification to the sacrifices of those of us, who that day in Senate stood our ground for them and for posterity.

Chapter 10

The Faculty of Engineering Today [32]

Since its inception, the Faculty of Fngineering has grown to include disciplines other than the three major disciplines of Civil, Mechanical and Electrical Engineering authorized by Senate at its founding. The expanded faculty carries the name Faculty of Engineering and Architecture. Courses are currently offered for a four-year degree course leading to a Bachelor of Engineering degree (General), and a five-year Bachelor of Engineering degree with honours in each of the disciplines of Civil, Electrical and Electronics, Mechanical and Maintenance Engineering. Architecture and Mining are poised to take their places as full departments in the 2017/2018 academic year, after several years exploring options for their establishment. However, courses in Mining have been taught in the faculty since 2013, following approval by the University Senate in 2008.

Organizational Structure of the Faculty

As is the tradition, the Faculty is headed by a Dean of Faculty who supervises all the constituent departments. The day-to-day running of the departments, is the responsibility of Heads of Departments appointed by the university on the recommendation of the Dean and approval by the Deputy Vice Chancellor of the University and Head of Campus of the college.

Entry Requirements into the Faculty

Entry requirements for the degree programmes are five WASSCE/GCE "O" Level credits including English Language, Mathematics, Physics, Chemistry, obtained in not more than two sittings. For entry into the Faculty at Year II, students must, in

112

addition to the requirements for entry into Year I, obtain at least two GCE Advanced Level passes in the London GCE/EDEXCEL examinations chosen from Physics, Chemistry, and Mathematics. There is now provision for admission directly into Year II, for applicants with faculty approved level of passes at the Higher National Diploma level examinations set by the National Council for Technical and Vocational Awards. This link with other institutions taking national diplomas, attempts to apply concepts of the national engineering training structure developed and proposed in 1971 when the faculty was about to be established.

Courses Offered and Structure

The faculty now runs a modular programme in line with other faculties of the University of Sierra Leone. Courses are taught in two semesters instead of three terms as in previous years. Since the faculty's inception, successive deans, and heads of department, have made every effort to make all academic courses relevant to local conditions and prevailing situations in the engineering job market. Their main objective has been to transfer knowledge that will result in the production of graduates of internationally acceptable standards, capable of adapting their knowledge to local technological conditions and the physical and socio-economic environment. Their graduates are expected to institute and promote change wherever they find themselves and the more capable, to be able to contribute to the advancement of their chosen professions.

At Year I (first year) and Year II (second year), all engineering students offer the same courses (common courses) including introductory courses in mining engineering which are serviced by the three departments according to the academic bias of the courses. At Year III, students branch off to any of the three departments according to their performance at Year II reflecting their academic bias. Thus, specialization in any of the disciplines commences at Year III. At the end of Year III, students' performances are assessed against certain criteria to determine whether they have qualified for the honours programme, including mining. Those who satisfy the minimum criteria in terms of Grade Point Average, proceed to Honours I (Year IV) and thereafter to Honours II (Year V). At the end of this year they take the final examination for the B.Eng. Honours degree. Students, who fail to meet the criteria at the end of Year III, proceed to the final Year IV Class where they graduate with a General Bachelor of Engineering Degree (B. Eng.).

There is an Industrial attachment programme for all students in the honours stream. These students are assigned to various industries at the end of Year IV. They commence their attachment in July and spend five months in practical hands-on training in areas of their respective disciplines. Students return to campus in December to complete their course work in Year V. The faculty is currently studying modalities and timing, to involve the general degree students also in the industrial training programme.

Post-Graduate Training at the Faculty

The faculty provides opportunities for post-graduate training in all its three main disciplines, Civil, Mechanical and Electrical Engineering. Students can undertake research leading to the awards of M. Eng and Ph. D degrees.

In the mid-1980s, the Department of Mechanical Engineering joined other universities in Africa in the UNESCO/UNDP sponsored regional programme entitled 'The African Network of Scientific and Technological Institutions (ANSTI')'. The aim of the network, was to develop learning/teaching materials for the adaptation of engineering education (DELTMEE), to local conditions. In addition to producing books in basic engineering subjects, the programme embarked on training for master's degrees in different aspects of engineering, based on identified expertise in member institutions. The programme was successful in stimulating regional cooperation in engineering education, training, and research in Africa. The Department of Mechanical Engineering was selected to undertake the masters programme in Industrial Engineering and Management (IEM). For over five years, the department enrolled students from all over Africa for these courses which lead to the award of the Master of Engineering (M. Eng) degree in Industrial Engineering and Management. By the time the programme ended in 1990, over 30 graduates had been trained in this area of specialization by the faculty. The faculty continues to expand its post-graduate programmes. Among new initiatives is a two-year M. Phil programme in Energy Studies, which is proving popular among students.

Prospects and Responsibilities

The faculty sees itself as a centre for stimulating talent and creating the conditions where innovation could thrive. Interaction among staff of different disciplines is encouraged. The faculty is aware of its responsibilities in training the nation's engineering manpower. It is committed to meeting those responsibilities, and overcoming difficulties which had militated against the achievement of its full role within the community, and the engineering profession. It believes that its reputation depends on its achievements in the following areas of its obligations:

- team management skills of the dean and heads of department;
- continuous staff development;
- quality of the teaching and learning environment; and
- co-ordination between faculty, college and university.

It understands that the resource pool of the university is small and demands on it are huge. It is acknowledged that the faculty holds the key to expanding that pool through attracting research and consultancy contracts. Its effort in that direction has yielded some results. Individual experts in the faculty are frequently consulted on technical matters by engineering consulting firms, industry, and government. However, much remains to be done and will need stronger recognition by the government that some of the investigations required by its technical ministries could be contracted to the faculty. In addition, the government could also

115

outsource to the faculty the review of technical recommendations it receives from foreign experts on important development schemes.

Chapter 11

The Slow March Towards Change

Expansion of Facilities and Programmes

The move towards expansion of facilities and programmes in the Faculty of Engineering at Fourah Bay College (FBC), the University of Sierra Leone's oldest college, was again the story of foresight and determination. Those elements in leadership were responsible for delivering the desired changes, which the faculty could celebrate today. Long-awaited programmes in architecture and mining were realized, increasing the range and scope of course offerings in disciplines other than the humanities. Like the hard march towards the establishment of the faculty years earlier, the achievement of the expansion of the faculty's programmes required leadership that rose above despair. The deans who fought to bring about these desired changes, explored every avenue, defied every obstacle to achieve their goals. Three deans who served the faculty at the material time were Dr. Wilfred E. A. Lisk, Professor Ogunlade Davidson and Ing. Badamasi Savage. Professor Davidson was instrumental in the revival of the proposal to establish a faculty or department of Architecture, made to the university by the Sierra Leone Institute of Architects (SLIA), in 1983, when Professor Ibrahim was Dean of the faculty. When Dr. Lisk succeeded him, he continued the effort to mobilize support within the university for the proposal, and maintained links with members of the SLIA, who were soliciting support for the training within and outside the country. However, timing of the presentation of the proposal for consideration by the university, seemed inappropriate then, and as a result, the proposal was shelved. When Professor Davidson took up office as Dean in 2004, he faced enormous obstacles in trying to resurrect the abandoned proposal. In the end, he developed a new one and brought together a team of likeminded scholars and architects to

117

study it, and advance its acceptance by the university. However, it was Ing Badamasi Savage, Dean Davidson's successor, who advanced the stages of proposal review and negotiations, that led to the achievement of a fully operational Department of Architecture.

In the case of the other significant change, it was Dean Savage who, during his term of office, had to face this added challenge: to address the country's emerging manpower needs in the mineral resources sector by implementing. a mining engineering programme. He embraced the complexity of the task with vigour, defying disappointments and delays that threatened to derail the process. It was,through his leadership that the 2010/11 academic year saw mining established as a discipline within the faculty, and taught to degree level.

The establishment of Architecture and Mining in the faculty was an achievement attained through dedicated leadership and years of determined efforts by many committed professionals, and university scholars. They helped to solicit local and international support for the establishment of these courses and facilities, and for the necessary training. The journey to this stage of development was long and trying in every respect, and is detailed in the sections which follow.

Vision and Drive towards the Training of Architects

The idea of training architects locally sprang from the concern of leading members of the Sierra Leone Institution of Architects (SLIA). In the shortage of architects in the country during and after the civil war years of the 1990s, sub-professional draughtsmen were passing themselves off as architects, becoming not only a threat to the image of the profession, but also endangering lives, property, and the environment. The war had itself left a legacy of devastation; the environment and the infrastructure suffered alarming destruction. When it ended, immense pressure was upon the grossly inadequate number of architects, resident in the country, to meet the challenges of reconstruction. Up to that point, all the architects in

Sierra Leone had been trained overseas, most of them under some form of grant or scholarship hardly available to today's school leavers. Moreover, the overwhelming majority of former architecture students had failed to return to the country on completion of their studies. As a result, only twenty-five professional architects were known to be in active practice in a country of 5.5million people. The situation became so serious, with repercussions on capacity, succession, and sustainability, that action had to be taken to halt the looming catastrophe in the profession.

The objective of training architects is to instill in prospective graduates, the necessary skills to take on the responsibility of shaping the environments in which the populace spend their daily lives. The county's budding architects should be endowed with the imagination to create the buildings and cities society needs to keep pace with progress. Architecture is much too important to leave to unqualified persons, because its forms and concepts reflect the nature of society of which they are a feature, and ultimately affect the way that society develops. This means that the nation requires architects who can respond to the different needs and values of the community they serve. An architect's skills are relevant to all aspects of the built environment, from constructing new buildings to conserving old ones. Architecture is a demanding profession that deals with many important issues today; for instance, exploring new ways of living, investigating new technologies and materials and ensuring that what is built is environmentally sustainable. It means also that an architect must learn a whole range of skills, even crossing the traditional boundaries between art and science, and applying them within national cultural and environmental contexts.

It was at the Inaugural meeting of the African Union of Architects (AUA) held in 1983, that the setting up of a school for training architects locally was first suggested. The SLIA's delegation comprised Arch. Jarrett-Yaskey, Arch. Jalloh Jamboria, Arch. I. N. Yillah, and Arch. Carlton-Carew. One of the key issues discussed at that meeting was the need to train architects within the region, as the cost of training them outside the continent was becoming

119

prohibitive for most African countries. Of more serious concern to planners was, that the majority of students trained abroad, preferred to remain where they had been trained, particularly those who studied in the United Kingdom and the United States of America. Encouraged by the interest shown at the meeting for local training in member countries, on their return home the Sierra Leone delegation devoted time and energy to mobilizing support within their professional body for reversing this regrettable trend.

In 1985, the SLIA decided that it was time to examine the possibilities of establishing a School of Architecture at Fourah Bay College, a constituent college of the University of Sierra Leone. Contacts with the university were made to achieve this objective. As Vice Chancellor of the university at the time, I and the Faculty of Engineering, welcomed the approach. A committee was appointed to study the idea and make recommendations. The committee was headed by Dr. Wilfred E. A. Lisk, then Dean of the Faculty of Engineering at Fourah Bay College (FBC). Membership was drawn from the university and the SLIA. The committee favoured the establishment of a school of architecture and recommended that the proposed staffing of the school include additional expertise recruited from outside Sierra Leone to strengthen the teaching pool. The committee then embarked on consultations to obtain the necessary overseas support for the budding initiative.

The Nigerian Institute of Architects (NIA) and the Commonwealth Association of Architects (CAA) were contacted. Both institutions were willing to support the initiative and recommended the appointment of a consultant, Professor Adeyinka Adeyemi. He was an expert in the training of architects, and had been involved in the establishment of several architectural schools in the sub-region. Professor Adeyemi agreed to come to Sierra Leone at the expense of the CAA and NIA. Unfortunately, his trip had to be cancelled and considerations of establishing the School of Architecture deferred, because the university was in the process of establishing the College of Medicine and the after paying the necessary subscription. Sierra Leone Law School. The additional commitment

120

to establish at the same time a School of Architecture, was thought to be too onerous for an administration then reeling under criticism for engaging in faculty expansion that some believed would cripple the university financially.

While waiting for the University of Sierra Leone to resume consideration of the proposal for the establishment of the School of Architecture, the SLIA continued to search for assistance from other overseas institutions. In 1996, contact was renewed with the Commonwealth Association of Architects (CAA). The CAA insisted that in order to be eligible for assistance, the SLIA first needed to become a member. The SLIA applied for membership and, after paying the necessary fee, was accepted only to discover afterwards that the CAA could offer no assistance towards the establishment of the school. It, however, advised that the SLIA contact the Commonwealth Universities Commission Fund for Technical assistance and also the European Union, both institutions better resourced to offer assistance. The approach to the Commonwealth Universities Commission Fund was made at a time in the mid-nineteen nineties when internal conflict was tearing Sierra Leone apart. Even the country's long-time development partners were withdrawing aid, preferring to wait until the conflict was resolved, before committing themselves to helping national causes, no matter how deserving. Consequently, very little progress was made in advancing the initial work done to establish the school during this period.

With the end of the conflict, came the surge of activity to address the devastation it had caused. Restoration of landmark buildings and reconstruction of the homes destroyed had to be carried out with the utmost speed, using the limited number of architects who had not left the country for safe sanctuaries in neighbouring countries and beyond. As With the acute shortage of efficient architects, the need for locally rained architects became even more urgent, and the establishment of the School of Architecture assumed a high priority. It was realized that there was a need not only to train architects but also technicians and draughtsmen.

Fortunately, the training of technicians and draughtsmen had long been carried out at the Freetown Technical Institute, now integrated into the Milton Margai College of Education, and Technology (MMCET). It was expected that after the establishment of the School of Architecture, a review of the MMCET curriculum would be necessary to upgrade the courses to a level permitting students who passed their final diploma examinations with good grades, to gain admission to the School of Architecture with certain course exemptions. Thus MMCET would become an important source of candidates for admission to the proposed school.

Responding to the post-conflict realities, the SLIA renewed attempts at seeking international support for the establishment of the school. At the same time, the alarming paucity of trained architects, most of whom were aging, prompted the resumption of the discussions with the university. In 2004, the then Dean of the Faculty of Engineering, Professor O.R. Davidson, prepared a draft proposal for the setting up of facilities for the training of architects within the Faculty of Engineering. The proposal received a favourable reaction from the University Senate. The central thrust of the proposal was to train students for a Bachelor's degree in architecture (B. Arch) at Fourah Bay College), with the active support of SLIA in the first instance, and later for the Master of Architecture (M. Arch) degree, perhaps outside of Sierra Leone, to enable the graduates to qualify for professional registration. The proposal included a change in the name of the Faculty of Engineering to the Faculty of Engineering and Architecture. This was accepted by the University Senate and reflected in the revised University Act of 2005.

That same year, the institution applied for membership of the International Union of Architects (UIA). SLIA was granted temporary membership of the union. Armed with that status, the SLIA made known to UIA and AUA, its intention to commence local training of architects in Sierra Leone and sought their assistance. The UIA's initial response was negative, for its authorities felt that a school of architecture in Sierra Leone would not succeed. Reasons proffered to support this view included the country's lack of human and financial resources,, and the lack of local experience. To compound their fears, the architectural school in Senegal had around the time of SLIA's approach been closed, and the Togo/Lome School was experiencing financial constraints. The odds were against SLIA.

Eventually, SLIA convinced the UIA that Sierra Leone's case was different from the others, and that there was an urgent need in the country to train architects locally, particularly because the alternative of continuing with overseas training was costly and retrogressive. There were already in place in the country relevant academic programmes and staff within the departments of Engineering, Pure and Applied Sciences, the Social Sciences, and Law at Fourah Bay College, which are mandatory for architectural students. The advantage therefore existed to have cost-savings by sharing resources such as teaching staff and lecture courses. This way, the cost of recruiting staff for complementary courses would be avoided.

On the strength of SLIA's arguments, and the commitment from one of its council members, Arch. Femi Majekoudoumi of Nigeria, to give his personal assistance to the project, the UIA agreed to co-operate fully. Arch. Femi Majekoudoumi provided the funds to recruit a consultant to carry out the feasibility studies for establishing the school. Since Professor Adeyinka Adeyemi had already been proposed in 1986 by the NIA and CAA he was again invited to carry out the study. He arrived in Sierra Leone in July, 2004, to commence the study, and with the full cooperation of the university and Professor Ogunlade Davidson, then Dean of the Faculty of Engineering, was able to complete the work within the short period of time that he was in Freetown. He submitted his draft report to the SLIA and the university and, prior to his departure, a meeting was held to discuss it with representatives of those bodies.

The university then set up a joint committee with the SLIA to examine the report in greater depth and propose a project implementation strategy. The committee comprised the following members:

Prof. O R Davidson.	Dean of Faculty of Engineering, FBC
Ing. A.B. Savage	Head of Department of Civil Engineering, FBC
Ing. V.S. Kamara	Senior Lecturer, Department of Civil Engineering FBC (acting as secretary to the committee)
Arch. C. Carlton-Carew	Sierra Leone Institute of Architects (SLIA)
Arch. M. Garber	Sierra Leone Institute of Architects (SLIA)
Arch. J.M.B. Aruna	Professional Head, Ministry of Works, and President, SLIA
Architect Alpha Tejan-Jalloh	Principal, TEDA Consulting Architects
Architect G. Mason	Sierra Leone Institute of Architects (SLIA)

The joint committee's final proposal and recommendations were submitted to the University Senate for approval which was given in 2004. The central thrust of the proposal was that the university should undertake, as a matter of urgency, the training of architects to graduate level. Students would pursue the degree of Bachelor of Science in Architecture (B.Sc. Arch.) over a four-year period, as a first stage (Part 1) of their studies. Successful candidates would then proceed to the second part of the programme, to qualify for the Master of Science degree in Architecture (M.Sc. Arch). Both programmes would receive the active participation of SLIA. In addition to the degree courses, graduates would be required to serve two years in structured supervised practical training. The proposal also provided for a change of name of the Faculty of Engineering. It would become the Faculty of Engineering and Architecture, to reflect the inclusion of the new programme. It was anticipated that the school would start admitting students in the 2005/2006 academic year. However, although the committee worked assiduously to achieve this objective, the university was unable to secure funding for the school that year.

It would take two more years for another effort to be made to revive the 2005 proposal. In 2007, a new joint committee, headed by Ing. Alpha Badamasie Savage, who had succeeded Professor Ogunlade Davidson as Dean of the Faculty of Engineering, was appointed to advance this effort. Working with the new chairman of the SLIA Planning Committee, Arch. Alpha O. Tejan-Jalloh, the new joint committee took strides to re-launch the project, armed with a comprehensive business plan developed by Ing. A. B. Savage and Arch. Tejan-Jalloh. The business plan incorporated the following reports, design, and cost estimates:

- Report developed by Professor Adeyinka Adeyemi; with changes to reflect current thinking in architectural education;
- Report on the rehabilitation of the existing Engineering Faculty Drawing Office to accommodate the School of Architecture for the first two years of its existence, and transfer of the drawing office to a new location;
- The design of a new mezzanine floor in the Civil Engineering Department for use as the new Engineering Drawing Office, and
- Budget costs for item (ii) and (iii) and other ancillary cost items.

The new target date for commencement of courses, was set for the 2010/2011 academic year. The minimum requirements for starting

125

the school had been determined. Firstly, the Engineering Drawing Office had to be rehabilitated and expanded to accommodate at least two studios, offices, library, and ancillary facilities for the first two years of the school's life. Secondly, funds had to be sourced for the construction of a mezzanine floor in the Engineering Department building, for the relocation of the Engineering Drawing Office.

Setting themselves three years to achieve this, the joint committee and the SLIA, headed by its new President, Arch. Ibrahim Yillah, embarked on a new drive to seek funding and technical assistance. Throughout 2007, several approaches were made to friendly countries and institutions for assistance. Promises of support were received from the Nigerian High Commissioner, Hon. Godson Echegile, through the good offices of Arch. Abel Onomake, a member of the SLIA Planning Committee, and from the Egyptian Ambassador, Hon. Mahmoud Ezzat. The Ministry of Works, Housing and Infrastructure, the Ministry of Lands and the Environment and the Ministry of Education were approached and briefed on progress with the planning of the school. Arch. Yillah's team impressed on these ministries the necessity for government to give the school priority in its education budget allocations and in project submissions for donor assistance.

In August that same year, Alpha O. Tejan-Jalloh visited the Royal Institute of British Architects in England and held fruitful discussions with the Director of Education, David Gloster. Nick Wilson, an architect, and Sebastian Wood, an engineer, facilitated the meeting. The Royal Institute of British Architects (R.I.B.A.), under the Presidency of Sunard Prasad, was keen to support the school. Because of this meeting, the R.I.B.A facilitated moves to link SLIA with Article 25, a UK registered charity that manages sustainable architecture projects in the developing world. Between July and August, 2008, the Executive CEO of Article 25, Victoria Wilson and Robin Cross, Director of Article 25, a Member of Parliament in the United Kingdom, and an Architect, visited Sierra Leone to collaborate with other stakeholders, including SLIA, the

126

University of Sierra Leone and Ministries, Departments and Agencies, to prepare a strategic plan, which would form the basis for soliciting funding for the proposed school. However, after this momentous start, progress stalled.

The 2010/2011 session came and went with little indication that the minimum provisions required for the school's establishment to proceed would be available. But the situation changed dramatically when, early in 2012, Fourah Bay College launched an appeal for extensive rehabilitation Consonant with the Sierra Leone government's plans to rehabilitate and upgrade the infrastructure of the country's public universities, the college received support for a proposal to be submitted to the Arab Bank for African Economic Development (BADEA), for a loan to fund the rehabilitation project.

By a stroke of good judgement and good fortune for the faculty's developments, Dean Savage, then newly elected to the post, was assigned the role of preparing the proposal for funding the Fourah Bay College rehabilitation project. He made certain that the construction of a building for a school of architecture was included in the scope of works. The proposal was successful and work commenced in the fourth quarter of 2016. The Fourah Bay College's rehabilitation and expansion plans would make possible the construction of Phase 1 of the School of Architecture building. Additional funding would have to be sourced to complete the remaining phases. It was envisaged that the necessary structures would be completed for use by the 2016/2017 academic year.

By this time, the SLIA had elected a new executive, headed by Arch. Gibril F. Koroma. Fearing too long a delay in the starting date for the school, the executive committee made proposals to the university and Faculty of Engineering to start admitting students in the 2017/2018 academic year, while construction of permanent buildings continued.

The proposal involved the use of land adjacent to the Engineering Faculty Drawing office, along the main access to the faculty, for the construction of simple and inexpensive interim accommodation for the school. The design of these structures should be such that they could be easily erected, readily phased out, but still form a coherent whole. Land for this structure would be provided by the college. The university approved the proposal, on condition that supplementary funds were raised for constructing the temporary structures. The SLIA was determined to see this interim arrangement successfully implemented and therefore embarked on a fund-raising campaign. Through appeals made by its members, early in 2017, the association secured seed money from a Charity in the United Kingdom, to start building the structure to provide temporary accommodation for the architecture programme, while the BADEA-financed building is under construction. It is hoped that the temporary structure will be ready for the programme to commence in the 2018 academic year.

Navigating the undulating road to the training of Mining Engineers

The failure to include mining as one of the disciplines established in the faculty at its inception, was an unfortunate mistake for which the country is paying the price today, as it has to fill vacancies for professional engineers in the mining industry with foreigners.. Records show that less than 20 professional mining engineers are registered, and since half of them are nearing retirement age, within the next 5 to 10 years, that number will be reduced to single digits unless remedial action is taken. The situation has become critical, considering the mineral resources potential of Sierra Leone and the ongoing mining activities, yet training the required number of mining engineers overseas would involve costs beyond the financial capability of the country.

When Dean Savage took office as head of the Faculty of Engineering in 2006, he felt that this omission should be corrected and immediately made the production of mining engineers part of his vision. Within a year of assuming office he had embarked on fulfilling that pledge.

In 2007, as a council member of the Sierra Leone Institution of Engineers (SLIE), he initiated discussions on the need for a mining engineering department at Fourah Bay College. As a result of that discussion, the council, decided to form a joint committee comprising members of the Faculty of Engineering and SLIE, to prepare a proposal and road map for achieving this objective. It was also agreed that the collaboration of overseas universities offering mining engineering degree programmes, was necessary. The University of Mines and Technology (UMaT) in Tarkwa, Ghana was mentioned as a reputable institution for possible collaboration. Members of council made other useful suggestions on the way forward, notably, seeking professional guidance from Ing. Tani Pratt and Ing. Andrew Keili, experienced mining engineers, with a wide knowledge of training requirements for the industry.

In 2008, with the support of the then Deputy Vice Chancellor of Fourah Bay College, Professor J. A. S. Redwood-Sawyerr, communication with UMaT was established. Later that year, Professor Redwood-Sawyerr and Dean Savage seized the opportunity of a trip to a conference of the Ghana Institution of Engineers in Accra, to visit UMaT and hold face-to-face discussions with the university on possible assistance. in planning a degree programme for mining engineers. They travelled to Tarkwa from Accra by road, and under stressful conditions, but happily, their discussions bore fruit in the form of a Memorandum of Understanding between the University of Sierra Leone (USL) and UMaT. Signed by Professor Redwood-Sawyerr and Dean Savage on behalf of the USL, it established a formal link between FBC and UMaT. Further to signing, the parties agreed that cooperative work would start initially, with customizing the UMaT mining syllabus to fit into FBC's faculty structure. That completed, a mining degree programme, including curriculum and structure, was developed.

This was submitted to the University Senate and approved in May 2008, setting the stage for the programme's implementation. The original plan was to run it as a split degree programme, in which modules for the first two years would be taught at FBC. These would be basic engineering with introductory mining modules. Students who wished to pursue the mining degree would then complete the degree course at UMaT. It was expected that the government or industry would facilitate the UMaT trainng, by offering scholarships/sponsorships to students who opted for this leg of their training. Unfortunately, the programme stalled when Dean Savage's tenure ended. The new Dean could not drive the programme to its full implementation. Sadly, in the 2011 academic year, students, who had completed the second year of their split course, could not transfer to UMaT. because arrangements were never made for their move. In order to complete their degrees, they, regrettably, had to revert to the other options, Civil, Mechanical or Electrical Engineering. However, the established introductory mining courses at years 1 and 2 continued to be taught at the faculty.

Fortuitously, in 2008 when discussions were continuing with UMaT on the commencement of the mining programme, the then Minister of Mines and Mineral Resources (MMR), Honourable Osman Boi Kamara, was apprised of the moves being made. Coincidentally, there was a country representative of the UNDP based at his Ministry at the time, with responsibility to address issues of technical capacity and succession planning. The initiative had arisen because the ministry had realized that it was unable to recruit newly qualified Sierra Leonean mining engineers into the Ministry; there were no new graduates available either locally or from abroad. The Minister himself, was one of the few Sierra Leonean mining engineers in the country at the time, and he and most of his staff were approaching retirement. His impending retirement and that of several qualified mining engineers among a small core of professional staff at the Ministry, had brought home to him, that the ministry's ability to regulate mining activities in the country would be seriously undermined, unless more mining engineers were produced in the shortest possible time. When he was briefed about the university's plans, he quickly embraced them, realizing the benefits that could accrue from collaborating with his ministry.

That collaboration led to a meeting with the UNDP country representative, at which the minister, members of the FBC Faculty and SLIE, were present. The meeting discussed short, medium, and long term options to implement training programmes for mining engineers. In view of his ministry's impending manpower crisis, the minister was more eager than the university, to accelerate the process of implementation. Having initiated the idea, Dean Savage was prepared to galvanize every support that availed itself. The meeting assigned him the task of preparing a short-term plan for producing mining professionals. Savage found himself leading the drive to address this serious national problem. The objective was the provision of proficient mining engineers for the Ministry Mines and Mineral Resources within one year.

Dean Savage knew that there were courses, taught at the faculty, such as Geotechnics, Engineering Geology, and Surveying, which cut across the disciplines of civil engineering and mining engineering. The suggestion was put to the Minister and the UNDP representative that graduates with good civil engineering degrees could be put through a crash programme in elements of mining to make them competent mining engineers. However, FBC was not then in a position, to offer such a programme. As discussions with UMaT were ongoing, the opportunity was taken to propose to UMaT, as a favour to FBC, to provide the crash programme under the terms of the signed Memorandum of Understanding. With the approval of his Vice Chancellor, the Dean of UMaT, Professor Jerry Kuma, put together a customized six months' training programme in mining engineering, for selected civil engineering graduates from FBC.

Funds for the training came from the UNDP. The students performed so well, that Professor Kuma suggested making a case for them to be admitted straight into the Master's Degree

Programme, if funding could be made available. This idea struck Dean Savage as an opportunity to train staff, who would serve both the ministry and the university, for using this strategy, the mining programme at FBC could continue to its final graduate stage without recourse to training outside the country. Savage approached the MMR again, and convinced the minister that the suggestion from UMaT was an opportunity that should not be missed. With his persistence, and help of the UNDP Representative, funding for these students to continue to the Masters programme, was secured from a Sierra Rutile Mines fund, administered by the Ministry of Finance (MoF), the MMR, and the European Union (EU). It would support four of the students initially and, on their return, another three would follow. The four commenced their Masters studies in 2009, and graduated in 2011, with very high grades.

Thus, began the process of restoring the country's mining engineering capacity. The first four mining engineers currently occupy managerial positions at the National Minerals Agency. While these students were training at UMaT, a new dean assumed office who was unable to drive the mining engineering programme to its final stages. In 2012, the university became aware of this situation and, anxious to save the programme, invited Dean Savage to take over the faculty again with a view to moving forward all its stalled programmes. Along with this assignment, he was appointed assistant to Professor Gbamanja, a position he still holds. Savage quickly re-established contact with the MMR. A new Minister, the Honorable Alhaji Minkailu Mansaray, had by then been appointed. He upheld the commitment of his ministry to the training programme for mining engineers and gave the faculty every assistance. Particularly, he was instrumental in making all the mining companies in the country provide financial support for the resuscitated programme.

Since there were already four mining engineering graduates who could be appointed Associate Lecturers, the programme ran smoothly, without interruption. The structure of engineering programmes at the faculty permitted the inclusion of mining modules without modification. The first two years of common courses, including mathematics, physics, and chemistry, with an introductory course in mining engineering, would remain for mining students, as in the split programme approved by Senate in 2008. As with all engineering students, mining students would branch off to their chosen discipline in year 3. In 2013, the University Senate approved this programme. When it was launched, the mining programme was offered as a unit within the Mechanical Engineering Department, with supervision by the Dean of the Faculty and the Head of the Department of Mechanical Engineering.

The civil engineers who were converted to mining engineers at UMaT had already been recruited as Associate Lecturers in 2012 on their return from studies. The implementing strategy adopted, was to add a year at a time to the new mining programme, as more competent staff became available. In 2016, the department graduated its first batch of 12 locally trained engineers with the B. Eng (Hons; Mining Option) degree. Two of them graduated with First Class honours. The mining engineering programme is now fully established at the faculty. The second cohort of students graduated in 2017. By the 2018 academic year, the mining unit should be strong enough to be granted full departmental status. Currently, there are five mining engineering lecturers: two full time, including one PhD, three Associate Lectures, and one Research and Teaching Assistant, who graduated with a first-class honours degree in 2016.

Curriculum Review and Restructuring of the Faculty Programmes

In early 2014, Dean Savage, started discussions at the Faculty Board on the review of the entire curricula of the faculty and the restructuring of academic programmes. This was prompted by the realization that certain courses and programmes offered at the faculty, had become obsolete, and needed to be replaced by others to satisfy the requirements of the job market in Sierra Leone. This was supported by the result of a survey undertaken by Professor J.

A. S. Redwood-Sawyerr on the expectations of employers and their perception of the relevance of current programmes to the needs of industry.

Based on the needs assessment, catalogued in Redwood-Sawyerr's book, a proposal to carry out the curriculum review was submitted to Senate. Senate fully endorsed the proposal requesting all heads of departments to make recommendations to a Faculty Curriculum Review Committee, authorized to vet it, before submitting it to the Faculty Board for approval. By May 2014, the internal assessment of the submissions had been completed. The Dean with the assistance of the Faculty Administrative Assistant and the Heads of Departments, compiled the final vetted document to produce a new Faculty Handbook for the period 2015/16 to 2018/19. A validation workshop, was held at the British Council on 8th August 2014. Despite the State of Emergency in force during the Ebola epidemic crisis in the country, a wide section of the academic and industrial community took part. The document that emerged from the workshop was presented to Senate in 2015 and approved. Following its approval, the revised structure and curricula became operative in the 2015/16 session. Provision was made for students still taking courses under the old engineering programmes, to continue with them until they graduated. The old programmes would then be phased out. The new programme and structure have been in force for the last two years; details are provided in the References and Notes.

Chapter 12

Development and Prosperity: The Challenges for Sierra Leone [33]

It must be understood that the future prosperity of any nation depends on the strength of the foundation on which that future can successfully be built. Among the most important ingredients for constructing that foundation is education, followed by the determination to set goals and undertake the process of attaining them. This means that without the right type and quality of education and its continued expansion and improvement, no nation can achieve the meaningful development that generates prosperity. In the classical sense, education aims at developing and retaining qualities that promote and enrich the social and material lives of every citizen and provides the means of generating a nation's wealth. In the technical sense, it is the process by which society transmits accumulated knowledge, values, and skills from one generation to another, to provide for its material advancement. Emphasis on education and training in science and technology as a policy directive, has helped propel countries in the northern hemisphere into the dominating position of technology giants, producing new and incredible methods and machines to improve living standards, create wealth and increase happiness of their peoples.

That same drive and vision is required in those African states, which are still struggling to rise from the quagmire of dependency to face the challenges of the competitive world of knowledge. With the continuing improvement in the level of awareness in the region, of the benefits of science and technology, there can be no excuse for continuing to ignore the potential of Science and Technology as a combined vehicle for achieving rapid and sustainable development. Many may complain that the price of achieving this goal is too high and that poor nations cannot afford it, when the consequences of not being able to afford it are clear. Without the knowledge of science and technology in any nation, and without the ability to harness their power, there will be only a life fashioned after stale and irrelevant models and lived in uncertainty and fear.

In Sierra Leone, the achievement in diversifying higher education to include training in science and engineering was a first step in a transformation that needed stimulus from government and industry to enable it to take advantage of existing internal and external opportunities. Within the country, employment opportunities were being created in existing and new businesses. Highly skilled manpower was in demand to fill skills gaps in every sector of the economy. The greatest shortage was in middle-level and high technology skills. These gaps had reduced the country's potential for attracting the foreign investment flooding into other newly independent countries, where the skills needed for operating commercial and industrial enterprises existed prior to their political independence and had been expanded since.

The years following political independence, had seen some significant efforts being made to achieve improvement in the educational sector, with focus on basic education. Insufficient attention had been paid to the development of higher education generally and particularly, to the growth of new science and technology institutions established in the wake of the founding of the engineering faculty at Fourah Bay College. The slow progress in strengthening and expanding the capability to train human resources at higher skills levels, has highlighted the enormous problems associated with the government's desire to exploit the nation's natural wealth and attain the developmental goals in the shortest possible time

These goals cannot be achieved without a concerted effort. The stage should be set right now for stimulating more creativity, increasing agricultural and industrial productivity and expanding opportunities for enhanced job creation; for preserving the environment and working towards the effective delivery of high quality public services in the areas of health, education, shelter, transport and food sufficiency. Educating and training a larger number of competent engineers is a vital part of the drive to bring about the change that is needed. But there is another part to change which, in the context of sustainability, requires it to be fundamental, not cosmetic. Development should be all embracing.,It should raise awareness at grassroots level, that poor conditions do not have to be permanent, and that all citizens can contribute to the change they desire and deserve.

While engineers are required to play their role in providing equipment and facilities to improve quality of life, the people, must in turn understand how to secure the continuing usefulness of these products. And that has a price; the proper education and training of engineers beyond the acquisition of world class technical skills should go hand in hand with the ability to work with communities, and help them assume ownership of the equipment and facilities provided for their benefit and be proudly protective of them. Of course, beyond this prescription comes method, that is, how to give ideas legs. It is often the 'how' that causes the most difficulty. The desire for improvement,often dies in the exhaustion that overcomes us when we try to implement what is required, and find that we must face the reality of what is possible.

Nevertheless, every effort should be made to champion reforms with the same compelling urgency as existed at the dawn of independence, when the new leaders of the country wanted rapid progress, and he idea spread that a modern state would evolve within fifty years as a result of the government's dynamic strategic plans. There is no doubt that the destinations envisaged in any reform should be determined with a clear vision of the future, tempered by the realism derived from an in-depth analysis of prevailing and projected economic circumstances.

There is a complementarity between education, development and prosperity which could be termed elements of national progress. In, this sense, it can be argued that the material advancement of any nation can be judged by the strength of the links holding these elements together, as much as by the effectiveness of each of them as a reliable complement. Thus, a high quality of domestic education is necessary to produce the skilled labour that attracts high financial investments to establish productive industries and promote domestic development. This in turn, creates high and durable domestic prosperity. It is easy to deduce from this argument therefore, that a poor domestic education can only create the opposite. Sierra Leone, like other countries in Africa, has been slow to realize that it must set its education and levels of skills attainment sufficiently high to attract meaningful investment for development. Often that scale of investment can only be sourced from foreign countries, as local capital has been difficult to generate within a poor earning environment.

Of course, there are economic and political realities which could hinder the formulation and successful implementation of policies to produce manpower with the highest level of desirable skills. The economic realities the nation faces, are the greatest setback to funding successful policies, and the failure of governments to internally mobilize the necessary capital for investment in revolutionary education policies. Without changing the culture of society that stifles the aspirations and energies of ordinary people to create wealth, the nation will continue to struggle to raise the capital for investment from within its borders. In this environment, it has been the individual institution that appears to take on most of the responsibility for raising the funds required, to meet the challenges that national development and global opportunities present.

Sierra Leone's national institutions figure poorly in global competitiveness in areas of economic growth and development. Yet one of the main drivers of progress in these areas, higher education and training, is being given less of a priority than it deserves. That has to change. The country needs to build confidence in its capacity to change direction and reset goals to achieve higher competitiveness in a world that recognizes only the highest standards in every activity that enhances development. Creativity and originality have become the qualitative standards by which higher education institutions are now mostly judged. Even as academic institutions in Sierra Leone aspire to achieve the highest endorsements based on these standards, they seem to lack many of the academic tools needed to keep abreast of them.

These are current challenges universities face, but they have made many of them conscious of the stiffness of the competition to be classed in the top league of the world's academic institutions. The goal for higher education should therefore be the transformation of our universities and colleges into institution known to produce the highest quality of graduates, and the highest standards of research. They will also be known for the highest reputation of academics on their staff lists, and the appropriateness and reach of their community services. Resident staff should welcome change and promote its implementation.

Many citizens of good will continue to hope for a new era of prosperity for their country, in which higher educational institutions will see a phenomenal growth in their scholastic reputation; an era in which they will be embraced with pride by a people who do not want them to fail, and who will be willing to support their development plans and give them financial support, individually, or as concerned groups of citizens, private entrepreneurs and alumni. Sierra Leone has a pool of talent both within the country and in the diaspora, from which it could draw expertise to help devise funding strategies and provide staffing options to accomplish this monumental task. They will have to deal with certain basic features of the existing situation in higher educational institutions.

Firstly, in respect of funding, institutions supported by the government do not enjoy total funding of budgets, which are already too low to provide the number and quality of staff needed to meet basic teaching and research commitments. Since there is no likelihood that it can fund any future transformation strategy, the government has given the national universities the freedom to seek additional funding from other sources while it pursues its agenda for change and prosperity.

Secondly, poor conditions of service and poor teaching and learning facilities have made it difficult to retain staff with high academic credentials. To overcome this problem, special academic staff support schemes need to be established. If well run and publicized, they should generate sufficient funds to supplement university salaries and provide an enabling environment for staff.

Thirdly, the quality of many of the products of the nation's tertiary institutions now fall well below recognized international standards.

Fixing these problems will require the implementation of an exceptional recovery plan which should be diversified and expanded with little dependence on government for the needed capital.There have been many strategies suggested by planners to diversify and increase funding to the national universities and other government supported tertiary institutions. One thing is clear. In every case, in every strategy chosen, what will oil the passage of the needed funds from source to point of delivery, is confidence in the recipient. That is, the institution's capacity to achieve its stated goals with the financial assistance provided. And this will be the rub. An institution seeking private financial assistance, must convince donors of its worthiness to be supported by showing the steps it is taking to renew its image and perform as a reputable citadel of learning.

Cramped accommodation, the most basic of equipment, and course curricula on the fringes of the nation's manpower requirements, do not produce professional engineers capable of responding to the need for innovative solutions to the myriads of problems facing the country, including its inability to exploit the mineral resources with which it is endowed. The present situation also does little to fulfil the desire of young and ambitious academics to engage in the pursuit of new knowledge, and join in the excitement of mastering and manipulating new technologies for the good of their nation.

High intellectual pursuits in targeted institutions must be accompanied by the physical transformation of the campuses themselves.

In proposing a strategy for the transformation of existing institutions into highly reputable ones, it has to be accepted that success in implementation will come only if those who carry them out sincerely wish them to succeed. Of course, beyond this wish comes method; that is, how those implementing changes get them done. It is often the application of devised methods that baffle, frustrating guaranteed outcomes and making what is achieved less than seemed possible at the outset. In this respect, strategies used in the training of engineers to function competitively in fast changing technological world, could equally be used in the training of high quality workforce in other disciplines.

Some planners have suggested that planning to achieve success, requires that it is done in a way similar to planning a journey. In starting a journey, a traveler must first decide where he wants to go. Then, he makes certain of the location from which he intends to start his journey. Next, he determines the distance between where he is and where he wants to go. Following that, he decides his mode of travel and the obstacles he is likely to encounter in the journey. Finally, he assesses the cost and time required to reach his destination. In the case of engineering training, the destination is the goal that should be reached. That is, 'to replenish and increase the pool of high quality engineers with the relevant training for the future advancement of their country'. The present position from which standards should rise, is the country's poor engineering capacity, reflected in the statistics of shortages and weaknesses, reported in the Human Development Reports between 2014 and 2016. They show that the expenditure on education as a percentage of GDP was 2.72. Viewing this figure with the most optimistic eye, it is easy to see how inadequate the investment in engineering education was. The consequence of that poor investment is reflected in the percentage of the population in poverty. At 72.68%, we can see the immensity of the task that lies ahead to match those of the country's neighbours. The figure for Ghana was 30.46, Nigeria 43.29, Ivory Coast, 59.33 and The Gambia, 60.77. Although they had escaped the devastation of the 2013-2014 Ebola scourge, these figures should clearly not be those the country should aspire to match.

What the traveler needs to find out next, is the distance between where he is and where we he wants to go. This is the gap that needs to be filled, to achieve the intended goal. Current standards are far from the goal that must be reached. In every area of engineering activity, it could be seen that there is a huge gap to close. Planners need to know all the elements that make up this gap, using manpower surveys or needs assessment. If carried out properly, it should bring out clearly the size of the deficit in quality and in the quantity of qualified engineers, as a percentage of the population. It will provide information on the number of institutions needed to train the numbers required over a period, the complement of equipment, lecturers and researchers required. It will give an indication of the state of the enabling environment, such as, ready outlets for products from training institutions, the effectiveness of professional engineering bodies regulating engineering practice, and their role in promoting continuous professional development. These will constitute the distance to be covered in the journey to effect the desired transformation.

The next stage of planning for this exceptional journey, is choosing the mode of travel, the method of getting to the destination. It can become a dilemma for planners to find a method that will succeed because there may be resistance to innovations. Also, some methods may appear too elaborate to attract support. In fact, the responsibility for devising and implementing any method for reaching the desired destination must be assigned to visionaries who can see the attainment of the goals set as a progression of competences from one stage to another, and can plan accordingly. The outcome envisaged should be the impact of quality output on the lives of every citizen in the short and long term. They should also view the vehicle for undertaking the journey, as one with two compartments, namely, sensitization, and action. Consideration should also be given to the possibility, that each will be susceptible to obstacles that may prevent the journey being completed, either in whole or in part.

The component of sensitization is the more critical of the components of the vehicle in which to make the journey, for it involves the management of a body of stakeholders and donors, to whom a consistent message should be communicated, emphasizing the desperateness of the existing situation, the need for transformation and its projected impact on the nation's development. Through this process, a group will be assembled, whose members will have expressed willingness to support a drive to act on receipt of proposals for financial and other assistance. The second component of the vehicle is the work plan. This is where the work to be done must be outlined. These actions, short and long term, should be prioritized; classed in order of urgency and cost. Short term action may include bringing graduate output, research activities, and staff and facilitates to an acceptable first stage level. Long term plans will focus on raising standards and quality of products, so they can compete in a fast-changing world dominated by spiraling technological discoveries. Some disciplines may not be as important as they once were; they should be replaced by new ones, or, in some cases, new courses within existing disciplines. Since not all could be covered at once a start should be made with skills required by the local market. A larger number of qualified lecturers will be needed, with a projected staff/student ratio permitting easier interaction with students at tutorials.

Students will be the beneficiaries of these improvements. Account should, therefore, be taken of their expectations in terms of job prospects and societal recognition. On completion of their studies, most of them will go into industry where they will encounter employers unforgiving of incompetence. They will be going out to work in communities which will hold them in high regard, or otherwise, depending on their knowledge and skills. Their training should equip them to meet these challenges through curricula geared towards developing skills in design, creativity, problem solving, modelling, assessing, and making economic choices, and in collaboration with industry, with new approaches to course delivery such as phasing and duration of programmes. Courses in entrepreneurship should be part of all engineering programmes, and policies in place to ensure that graduates enter an industrial sector strengthened by monetary incentives, and opportunities to secure loans. These measures would promote private investment in infrastructure.

Another imperative, is to include in the early years of a student's training, courses in the humanities and social studies. Engineers must learn that as part of their community, their quality of life will be, as affected by the infrastructure they create and maintain, as anyone else's. They ought to be made aware of societal problems and the role they will be expected to play in solving them. Rather than adding to the lengthening chain of the government's responsibilities, they should aim to be part of the section of the population that creates employment.

The planners of any such transformation ought to be aware of obstacles to the achievement of a successful journey towards achieving the desired goal, including the human tendency to resist change out of fear of what might result, for example, loss of jobs and/or status. Another obstacle to success would be failure to achieve graduate targets, due to low quality admissions into courses. Not properly redressed, this situation could have a far-reaching effect on manpower quality. Furthermore, the attrition rate after qualification may be higher than projected. Planners may find that fewer opportunities exist for post-graduate practical training, as companies with enough experience to train graduates are becoming reluctant to accept trainees, some of whom abandon their training before acquiring all the skills necessary to make them proficient professional engineers. A more serious obstacle to reaching planned targets, will be the migration of qualified engineers to other countries, where conditions of service and quality of life are more attractive,. Less damaging to the country would be graduates who choose to retrain in order to enter more lucrative professions, or move into non-engineering positions in government. Over production of graduates may appear to be the way to overcome this, but could be counterproductive, leading to graduate unemployment. Any corrective measures would have to be given thorough consideration.

With the information assembled to undertake the journey, the final step should be estimating the cost of completion in accordance with priorities set. If well packaged, a plan incorporating the ideas expressed in the foregoing pages, will stand a good chance of attracting material and financial support, not only from institutional donors, but also from local and foreign philanthropists who would like to see Fourah Bay College of the University of Sierra Leone restored to the high esteem in which it used to be held in Africa and beyond.

.

References

1. El-Idrisi
2. Fyle and Abraham
3 Fyfe, Christopher: *A history of Sierra Leone,* London, 1962.
4. Fyle, Cecil Magbaily: *Historical Dictionary of Sierra Leone,* MD: Scarecrow Press, 2006.
5. University of Sierra Leone Act, 1972, pub. Government of Sierra Leone.
6. Margai, Sir Milton, Augustus Strieby, 1896-1964 - First Prime Minister of Sierra Leoene, 1961-1964.

7. Davidson Nicol, Principal of Fourah Bay College, 1960-68); Vice Chancellor, 1966-68)

8. Hyde -Forster , Latilewa – First female graduate of Fourah Bay College . The college's first female hall of residence was named after her. She became a Principal of the Annie Walsh Memorial School in Freetown, the oldest female secondary school in the country.
9. Leicester and Gloucester – Most villages in the Freetown Peninsula were named after English towns, a relic of their colonial past.
10. Mount Sugar Loaf – This is the highest mountain in the Freetown peninsula . Similar landforms in other parts of the world carry this name . Examples could be found in countries such as Brazil , Australia , Japan , the United Kingdom , and the United States of America.
11. See Report of the Conference of OAU African Ministers of Education September 1967 and UNESCO Conference on Education and Science 1968.
12 . This college was established as Njala University College independently from Fourah Bay College and admitted students of Agriculture and Education for studies leading to the award of degrees.
13. Fisher Cassie; Formerly Professor of Civil Engineering, University of Newcastle-upon-Tyne. He is the author of several books and articles on Structural Engineering and The Mechanics of Engineering Soils.
14. Landour – Formerly Professor of Chemistry at Fourah Bay College
. 15. Bates– Formerly Professor of Botany at Fourah Bay College.

16. Zulouf– Formerly Professor of Mathematics at Fourah Bay College.

17. Sawyerr, Harry – Formerly Principal of Fourah Bay College (1968-1973). Clergyman, educationist and author; Pro Vice Chancellor, University of Sierra Leone (1970-1972); Canon of St George's Cathedral, Freetown (1961-1964) . On retirement from Fourah Bay College, he was appointed Principal of St. John's College, Barbados.

18. Porter, Arthur Thomas – Historian and writer. First full-time Vice Chancellor of the University of Sierra Leone (1974-1984). Principal, University College Nairobi, University of East Africa and later Vice Chancellor of the University of Nairobi. He is the author of several published works including *"Creoledom, A Study of the Development of the Freetown Society"*

19. Jones Eldred Durosimi Jones– Literary critic and author of several literary works. Formerly Principal of Fourah Bay College (1974-1985); Pro Vice Chancellor of the University of Sierra Leone. He was editor of African Literature Today and series editor of "New Perspectives on African Literature".

20. Edward Blyden III– Formerly Dean of the Faculty of Arts, Fourah Bay College; Head of Department of Political Science and Diplomacy and the Department of African Studies University of Nigeria, Nsukka (1960); diplomat, political scientist and educator. He was Ambassador Extraordinary and Plenipotentiary from Sierra Leone to the Soviet Union, and accredited to Romania, Poland, Yugoslavia, Bulgaria, Czechoslovakia and Hungary (1971-1973); Sierra Leone's Permanent Representative to ambassador to the United Nations (1974-1976). Was awarded the Peace Medal by the UN Secretary of State (1980).

21. The paper referred to was later published under: Evans, R. H. and Thomas, K. *"Shear Effects in beams reinforced with special steel bars"* Civil Engineering (London) v 59 Nov. 1964.

22. Technical Conferences at which papers from members of staff of the Department of Engineering were presented, included the following: *Reliem Symposia on Concrete and Reinforced Concrete in Hot Countries; Conferences on Engineering Education in Middle Africa; Rehovot Conference on Science and Education in Developing States; Biennial Conferences of the West African Science Association; International Conference on Appropriate Technology in Rural Societies.*

147

23. Evans, R. H.–Formerly, Professor of Civil Engineering and Administrative Head of the Departments of Engineering at the University of Leeds; Author of several books on reinforced an prestressed concrete; formerly, consulting editor to McGraw-Hill Book Company.
24. FSSU– This is the Federated Superannuation System for British Universities, and was a compulsory scheme made available to appointees at the University of Sierra Leone until it was suspended in the late 1980s.
25. Yilla, Idrissa – Former Lecturer in Civil Engineering.
26. Griffin, Abayomi – Former Chief Mechanical Engineer, and later General Manager of the former Sierra Leone Railways. He served as Part-Time Lecturer in Mechanical Engineering at Fourah Bay College from 1962-1969.
27. Aggrey (1879-1927) – The Hazen Foundation is an American based foundation which seeks to assist young people, particularly minorities. This fellowship is directed at African scholars seeking further advancement of their academic careers. It was named after Dr. James Emmanuel Kwegyir Aggrey, one of the leading figures in education in Africa. He was a great sociologist, orator, preacher and politician who fostered inter-racial cooperation. Many African scholars benefitted from this fellowship.
28. See Miles, L. M. *Harry Alphonso Ebun Sawyerr 1909 to 1986; Anglican Sierra Leone*; in Dictionary of African Christian Biography, 2005.
29. World Plan of Action – A United Nations initiative to promote the Application of Science and Technology to Development (1970).
30. See Palmer, Eustace, Holt, E, & Porter, Arthur T: Sierra Leone Educational Review: *All our Futures*: Final Report, University of Sierra Leone, 1976.
31. The Sierra Leone Institution of Engineers at their 2012 Biennial Conference passed a resolution recommending to Sierra Leone Government the enactment of an Industrial Training Levy.

32. Savage, Badamasi, "Faculty of Engineering," Faculty Paper, 2017

33 Koso-Thomas, Kosonike, *Consequences for Sierra Leone and its development,* Keynote Address to the Engineers for Change Conference on Post Ebola, London, 2015.

Notes

Revised Undergraduate Degree Programmes in the Faculty of Engineering & Architecture

Background/Justification

Engineering may be defined as a profession in which knowledge of mathematical and natural sciences, gained by study, experience and practice, is applied with judgment to develop ways to utilize, economically, the materials and forces of nature for the benefit of mankind. The Undergraduate Engineering curriculum has recently been revised with the help of industry stakeholders. Internal (USL) and external validation workshops have been held to receive input from the chief actors in Engineering and Engineering education in Sierra Leone.

A restructuring of the Faculty's curriculum means that students can now be accepted directly into the Department of their choice. This will facilitate introduction of more courses which are focused and will add value to the training of Engineers so that they are ready for work in Industry and ready to cope with emerging technologies.

The curriculum will now enable all students to undertake Industrial attachment (including Mining Engineering Students) during the second semester of year 4. Course work in year 4 will be completed during the first semester. Students will return towards the end of the second semester to complete the writing and presentation of their Industrial Report which will be properly supervised and presented as a module to carry 6 credit hours and take the place of a full dissertation as in the case of General students. Only Honours students will proceed to Honours 2 and do full dissertations. This will now solve the current situation in which the General Degree students are disadvantaged by not going for industrial attachment. Note that dissertation also would continue to carry 6 credit hours for all Departments.

The Curricula of all Departments have now been revised for presentation to the University. The proposed restructuring will now include steps to expose Civil Engineering students to the discipline

149

of Architecture so that they learn how to read Architectural Drawings and relate better with Architects in the field of building construction work. A course titled "Elements of Architecture I and II will be introduced in years 1 and 2 respectively. This hopefully will be a springboard to actualize the commencement of the proper Architecture programme which is long overdue. The Surveying course will now be titled "Surveying and Geo-informatics", so that GPS technology will be grasped. In the Electrical and Electronic Engineering Department, courses in Fibre Optics Technology for example, will be introduced. Under the revised curriculum, for the Honours students, there will be the main general courses at year 5, but specialist optional courses will be available from which a student can choose one or two to make up the required credit hours, but depending on the desired emphasis of the student. This will give flexibility to Honours students to obtain further/in-depth knowledge in areas of discipline that they may wish to specialize in at postgraduate level. Such courses, for example in Civil Engineering, could include Water Resources Engineering, Environmental Engineering (for which main stream Hydrology and Public Health Engineering courses will be prerequisites respectively), Geotechnical Engineering (for which mainstream courses in Soil Mechanics will be prerequisites), Highway Design, Highway Economics (for which mainstream Transportation Engineering will be a prerequisite).

Aim of the Programme
Engineering education at the Faculty of Engineering and Architecture is geared towards producing graduates who will be able to:
- Develop new products.
- Design and supervise the construction of new projects.
- Install and maintain complex plants.
- Make the best use of local resources in order to improve the economy.
- Advance the discipline of engineering education through research, development, and the training of engineers.

150

Profile of the Course

General Academic Information

The Faculty will now run a straight five-year Honours Degree programme in the following Departments and Engineering disciplines:

- Civil Engineering
- Electrical & Electronic Engineering
- Mechanical & Maintenance Engineering
- Mining Engineering

Generally, each programme comprises:

Basic Engineering Courses: These are courses taken in year one taken by all students entering the Faculty at this level. They are general foundation courses for all engineering disciplines. These courses also include science courses such as Physics and Chemistry as well as Mathematics, which are run by the Faculty of Pure and Applied Sciences. Civil Engineering students also offer courses in Geology from the Geology Department at some point.

Year two also comprises of Basic Engineering Courses and Mathematics; however, at this level, students begin to offer courses specific to their desired Departmental disciplines together with the Mathematics and Computer Aided Design Courses which are to be taken by all students at year two.

Core Engineering Courses: These are courses taken from year three to year five. The courses taken at these levels are professional engineering courses and are mainly offered at the various Departments in the Faculty.

Faculty courses: These are mandatory and are to be taken by all students in all the disciplines.

The Faculty runs a modular programme in line with the rest of the University of Sierra Leone. Courses are taught in two semesters each of 15 weeks. The course schedules for year 2 include: Mathematics and Computer Aided Design for all students, with the remaining modules being discipline-specific, and selected according to the

151

Department and discipline the student wishes to graduate in; therefore, for the other Departments, year 1 course schedules and descriptions are not repeated but year 2 courses are provided for each Department. The general educational objectives and Goals for each engineering Department are included in the Undergraduate course catalogue, which also provides brief course descriptions with lecture topics; detailed syllabi are to be developed from these course descriptions by individual lecturers based on the expected learning outcomes for the students.

The course descriptions are coded as follows:
- Course abbreviation and number.
- Course title.
- Parenthesized numerals e.g. (3-0-3) indicate, in order, the classroom lecture hours, the laboratory hours, and the semester credit hour value of each course.
- Courses coded FENG are common Faculty courses offered by all students in the Faculty

Auditing of Courses
Students may attend a course outside their prescribed programme. The course shall be recorded in their transcript only if they have registered for it with the approval of the Head of their Department and the Dean of Faculty. Students are required to attend classes of audited courses.

Departmental Elective Courses
Students should select 6 credit hours of elective courses at year five; the elective courses are courses which allow for some degree of specialization in one of the traditional areas of the disciplines in the respective Departments.
General Elective Courses
Subject to availability of time in lecture timetables, students may choose to take modules from other Departments in the Faculty or another faculty.

Students are required to pass such elective modules, as grades obtained shall be factored into the calculation of Grade Point Averages (GPA's).

Eligibility Criteria and Selection Process

To increase the quality of the freshman intake, it has been felt necessary to tighten the entry requirements, especially for Mathematics/Further Mathematics and Physics. It is hoped that if weak students are weeded out at this level, the quality of the Faculty's graduates will be enhanced.

Minimum Admission Requirements

1. The minimum admission requirement for entry into the Faculty are five credits at not more than two sittings in WASSCE or GCE "O" Level with the subjects combined into **three** categories for Admission to Year I as follows:

CATEGORY A	CATEGORY B	CATEGORY C
Maths/ Further Maths, English Language, Physics	Chemistry Science Core	Technical Drawing, Engineering Science, Computer Science, Biology, Geography

a) Candidates must obtain **Credit** of a minimum grade of **C5** in the three **Category A** subjects, except for English Language for which a minimum grade of **C6** is required.

b) In addition to the requirements in (a) above, candidates must obtain credit of minimum **C6** in at least one subject each from category **B** and **C**.

c) Candidates with 'A' levels:- candidates with the minimum of **5 "O" level Credits** including English language of **"C"** or better and with **Credits** of **"C"** or better in Mathematics and at least one **"A" level** subject chosen from **Physics and Chemistry,** will be admitted to **Year II.**

2. Candidates with **OND** and **Pass** at **HND** with minimum **C6** in English Language at **WASSCE** will be admitted to **Year II.**

3. Candidates with **OND** and **Credit or Distinction** at **HND** with minimum **C6** in English Language at **WASSCE** will be admitted to **Year III.**

4. Candidates with **OND** with a minimum **C6** in English Language at **WASSCE** will be admitted to **Year I.**

5. All **OND** and **HND** candidates with the entry requirements but without the minimum **C6** in English Language at **WASSCE** will be required to take and pass the College Matriculation English Language exam for admission.

6. Applicants with qualifications other than those listed above will be internally assessed at the Faculty for suitability for admission".

Index

A. R. Cusens, 104

Abayomi Griffin, 69

Akabi-Davies, 50

Alfred Sonah, 90

Arthur T. Porter, 61, 88

ASTRAD, 91

B. B. Ibrahim, 131

Bishop T. S. Johnson, 88

Brian Nicol, 44, 52, 64

Britain, 25, 30, 31, 56, 66, 68, 79

Church Missionary Society (CMS), 26

Civil Engineering, 39, 40, 131, 52, 57, 62, 65, 80, 86, 104, 110, 124

CMS, 26, 32

colony, 7, 13, 16

D. J. Ryley, 104

Davidson Nicol, 28, 31, 43, 45, 74, 82, 85

Department of Geology, 28, 37

Dr Minwarin Prescod, 39, 44

Dr. Magithia's, 44

Dr. Minwarin Prescott, 44

Dr. Prescod, 39, 44, 65

Durham, 13, 17, 26, 36, 37, 38, 64, 65, 82, 83

Edward Blyden III, 61, 85

Edward Jones, 43

Eldred Jones, 28, 61, 83, 84, 90, 91

Engineering , 15-17, 24, 28, 31-32, 34-42, 44-50, 52, 55-57, 59-62, 64-69, 72-74, 76, 78-83 , 85, 114, 115, 117, 120, 122, 127, 129, 130, 131, 134, 136, 137, 145, 178, 180

Fourah Bay College , 13-16, 26, 27, 31, 32, 34-38, 40, 41, 44-48, 56, 64, 65, 67, 68, 72, 79, , 82-85, 88, 89, 91, 99, 100, 110

Frank Fraser, 65

Freetown, 13, 21, 22-24, 26, 27, 37, 67, 82, 98, 99, 122, 123

General Certificate of Education, 100

George Lewis, 86, 87

Gloucester, 31

Guinea, 13, 27

Harry Sawyerr, 28, 61, 82, 85, 88

Henry Jones Alcock, 43

Hero, 50

Hon. N. A. P. Buck, 90

Hon. S. I. Koroma, 90

Idrissa Yilla, 69

Institute of Education, 34

Institute of Public Administration and Management, 34

Institution of Engineers, 100 103, 129

J. E. Houldin, 104

J. J. Grant, 43

John McCormack, 131

Kings College Newcastle-upon-Tyne, 36, 39, 65

Kortright, 52, 53, 74

Kosonike, 156
Lati Hyde, 29
Leicester, 31
Liberia, 13
Metcalfe Sunter, 43
Milton Margai College, 27, 122
Miss Nelson, 62
Miss Samson, 42, 43, 56
Mount Aureol, 27, 29, 47, 52, 67, 68, 74
Mr Albert Smith, 44
Mr. Richards, 65
Mrs. Carter, 62, 66
N. J. Garber, 105, 110
Nationalists, 11, 33
Nigeria, 10, 32, 46, 123, 142
Njala University, 34, 4,579, 88, 89
OAU, 95
Oni Gabbidon, 30
Oxford, 83
Professor Cassie, 72
Professor Derek Whittaker, 78

Professor Fisher Cassie, 40, 44, 66
Professor R. H. Evans, 67
Protectorate, 13
Saint George's Cathedral, 82
Samuel Adjai Crowther, 26
Samuel Bankolé Jones, 89
Samuel Burney-Nicol, 52
Seray-Wurie, 84
Sierra Leone, 6, 10, 13, 16, 17, 18, 23, 27, 30, 33, 34, 40, 43, 45, 46, 52, 63, 65, 66, 68, 69, 71, 79, 82, 83, 88, 89, 98, 100, 101, 103, 111, 113, 117-124, 126-129, 133, 136, 138, 139, 145
Sugar Loaf, 31
University of Oxford, 26
University of Sierra Leone, 187, 13, 17, 34, 40, 45, 68, 79, 82, 88, 139, 143, 146, 153, 155, 171, 173, 175
Wesleyan Missionary Society (WMS), 26
WMS, 26, 32
World Bank, 25, 95